Songs of the Rails by Alexander Anderson

Alexander Anderson was born on April 30th 1845 in Kirkconnel, Dumfries and Galloway, Scotland, the sixth and youngest son of James Anderson, a quarrier.

When he was three, the family moved to Crocketford in Kirkcudbrightshire where he attended the local school. Years later Anderson would take long walks in the surrounding hills finding inspiration for his poetry from both the stunning landscape and its local reputation for martyrdom.

At 16 he was back in his native village working in a quarry. Two years after that, in 1862, he switched careers to the railways becoming a surfaceman or platelayer on the Glasgow and South-western railway. He now used 'Surfaceman' as his pseudonym.

Anderson is recognised as one of Scotland's leading poets and, as a young man, he spent much time learning languages such as French, German and Spanish well enough so that he could immerse himself in their poetry and better the quality of his own.

By 1870 he was sending poems to 'The People's Friend' of Dundee.

In 1873 his first book, 'A Song of Labour and other Poems', was published by the Dundee Advertiser in a print run of 1000. With the support of The People's Friend the run sold out within two weeks.

The Rev George Gilfillan, a poetry critic in Dundee, was also effusive in his praise. He wrote to Thomas Aird saying: "You will be greatly interested in his simple manner and appearance—an unspoiled Burns is these respects and not without a little real mens divinor. Of course you know his poetry and his remarkable history".

Examples of his poems were also published in the many of the time's leading periodicals Good Words, Chambers's Journal, Cassell's Magazine, Fraser's Magazine and the Contemporary Review.

It was a good decade for him. Other poetry volumes were also published: 'Two Angels' (1875), 'Songs of the Rail' (1878), and 'Ballads and Sonnets' (1879).

In the following year he was made assistant librarian in the University of Edinburgh, and after an interval as secretary to the Philosophical Institution, which he seemed not to enjoy, he returned as Chief Librarian to the University.

Anderson would write no further volumes but would still occasionally contribute to periodicals and magazines.

Alexander Anderson died at his home in Edinburgh on 11th July 1909 at age 64.

He left behind a number of unpublished poems which were collected and published as 'Later Poems' in 1912

Some critics, in "reviewing" a former work of mine, took exception to the railway poems it contained, as being exaggerated in incident and over-drawn in treatment. In reply to these criticisms, I beg to remark that nearly all my railway poems are founded upon facts, and not a few of them upon incidents that have taken place upon a line on which I work. There are others founded upon accounts of railway accidents, seen in glancing over the papers in my leisure hours; while others, again, have for basis communications made to me by railway men with whom I came into contact in my daily work. I will frankly admit, however, to having taken advantage now and then—although in a very slight degree—of the license usually allowed to verse-writers of altering details in order to create a more complete whole.

One word more. I send out this volume, like former ones, in the hope that it may interest my fellow-workers on the railway, and heighten to some degree their pride in the service, however humble may be their position. I trust that its perusal may lead the engine-driver, among others, to look upon his "iron horse" as the embodiment of a force as noble as gigantic—a force which has opened up for commerce and industry a thousand paths that otherwise would have remained undiscovered: a power destined, beyond doubt, to be one of the civilisers of the world.

Index of Contents

MY READERS

A worker on the rail, where, day by day,
The engine storms along,
And sends forth, as he thunders on his way,
Wild strains of eagle song.

Or toiling on with heavy pant and strain,
As if within his breast
A god, bound by some splendid doom to pain,
Lies in his wild unrest;

And struggles like Enceladus, until,
Through all his shining length,
Each fire-fed sinew answers with a thrill,
And shakes and gleams with strength.

Then the wild vigour, shooting to its point
Of madness, fills each limb
That strides with one great sweep from joint to
joint
Of rails, that under him

Bend, as they feel his sudden certain grasp,
Or quiver as he reels,
And slips and slides with sullen grind and rasp
Of sternly-rolling wheels.

Or in the night, when darkness, like a veil,
Curtains the sleep of earth,
He flares along the pathway of the rail
Like a Titanic birth

Of some great monster from whose throat, as when
A new volcano wars,
A million sparks of fire burst up, and then
Fall down like mimic stars:

As with unwinking eye of glowing white
He tears the night apart,
And with broad spears of palpitating light
(The lightnings of his heart),

He shears the midnight with its shadowy shrouds,
Till every breath and pant
Mirrors and paints itself against the clouds,
Like northern lights aslant.

And swift as thoughts fling arches over space
In some worn giant's dream,
He rushes, crown'd with flame, upon his race,
The god of fire and steam!

Nay, when far out among the hills I lie
Beside the moorland streams,
Hearing them whisper forth with lulling sigh
Their little hopes and dreams:

He follows still, and from the distant bound,
His whistle echoes shrill,
Lapping with an invisible wave of sound
Each rift and shore of hill;

Or in the city, when I pace the street,
At one with all my kind,
Dreaming I hear in all the tramp of feet
The steady march of mind,

Moving to silent battles still unfought,
And seeing far on high
Standards, which truth with her own hands has wrought
For men to guard or die.

And hearing the firm tramp of peoples strong
In the high rights of man,
I move, as if one of the fearless throng,
A footstep from the van.

Till, worthy climax to my dreams, the black
Wild monster rushes on,
Along great arches that uprear their back,
Like Atlases of stone.

And linking surging street to street, he seems
Aglow with dusky scorn,
The swart apostle preaching wondrous dreams

Of days and years unborn.

For with him, like a prophecy that raves
Of some wild fruitful deed,
Go the great energies that kneel like slaves
Wherever men have need.

What marvel, then, that seeing, day by day,
The engine rush along,
That I send you, from out the "four-feet way,"
This book of railway song.

A SONG OF LABOUR

RESPECTFULLY DEDICATED TO MY FELLOW-WORKERS WITH PICK AND SHOVEL EVERYWHERE

Let us sing, my toiling Brothers, with our rough, rude voice a song
That shall live behind, nor do us in the after ages wrong,
But forever throb and whisper strength to nerve our fellow kind
As they rise to fill our footsteps and the space we leave behind.
What though hand and form be rugged? better then for Labour's mart—
I have never heard that Nature changed the colour of the heart—
For the God above hath made us one in flesh and blood with kings,
But the lower use is ours, and all the force of rougher things.
Then, my Brothers, sing to Labour, as the sun-brown'd giant stands
Like an Atlas with this planet shaking in his mighty hands.
Brawny arm'd, and broad, and swarthy, keeping in with shout and groan,
In the arch of life the keystone, that the world may thunder on;
Ever toiling, ever sweating, ever knowing that to-day
Is the footstool for the coming years to reach a higher sway.
Up, then, we, his rugged children, as the big hours move and pant,
For that cannot be but noble what he claims and cannot want:
Sing, and let his myriad voices bear the burden far along,
While we hail the mighty engine as the spirit of our song!

Arm to arm, and let the metals into proper range be thrown,
Let us smooth the iron pathway to the monster coming on.
Lo! he dawns adown the distance, and his iron footway rings
As he bounds, a wander'd meteor, muffled up in smoky wings—
Earth beneath his mighty footsteps trembles at the sudden load,
As of old the flood Scamander at the falling of the god.
Give him freedom, strength he needs not, only space and bound to fly,
As at night, in starry silence, glides a planet through the sky—
Thus he comes, the earth-born splendour, and with sudden shriek and gasp
On he flames, the Jove of Commerce, with the lightnings in his grasp.
O, my Brothers, this is something, in the fret and rush of days,

Worthy of our love and wonder, and the throbbing out of praise;
Then another wilder pæan for this march of thought and mind,
Some ecstatic dithyrambus that shall deify our kind.

Arm to arm, and let the metals into proper range be thrown,
Let us shape the iron pathway for the monster coming on;
Make his footing sure and steady, fitting for a thing like him,
Rolling out his seven-leagued paces smoother than a bird can skim ;
Welding city unto city, and as with strong withes of steel
Drawing traffic into method, till his muscles shake and reel;
Stretching out, Briareus-like, a hundred arms of sudden stroke,
Rolling upward to the darken'd heavens Python-coils of smoke;
Touching, like the gods of fable, all things into noble strife,
As before the heated sculptor flash'd the statue into life.
O, what strength shall be his portion in the coming reach of time,
When his sinews swell and ripen into firm and perfect prime,
He shall be the tireless monster that like Gulliver shall lead
Busy peoples to each other only with an iron thread.

Heart! but this grand world rolls onward through the shadows of the years,
Swift as fell the reckless Phæton headlong through the startled spheres;
And along with it we wrestle, shaping bounds we slowly reach,
For this knowledge is a master whose first aim is to unteach.
So, he moves with time and patience, working with a careful heed,
Growing more and more in earnest when he moulds the perfect deed;
Therefore guide him well, and listen to his slightest spoken word,
For a simple note will sometimes lead us to a fuller chord;
And the finish'd triumph with us shall a hundredfold repay
All the toil, and search, and panting for the source of purer day.
"But," says one, who still will murmur in the camp of brotherhood,
" Progress comes with tardy footsteps, and can do the grave no good."
There but spoke the Cynic, Brothers, curbing down with strongest steel
All the width of human purpose, all that brain can do and feel;
Scorning ever outward action, but to wrap himself in toils
Spun to catch the things that wither, spun to catch the dust that soils.
Shame on such! they are not worthy of the common breath they draw,
Since with it they make existence wither to a narrow law.
Wider range and freer action, nobler maxims for my breath;
I would wish my fellows success from the very jaws of death:
Death! a moment's cunning darkness flung across the trembling eyes
As we flash into the spirit cradled in a wild surprise.
Then what motions come upon us, golden laws of sudden calm,
Raining down eternal silence, raining down eternal balm.
Dare I fix my vision further, deeming that we mould this mind,
But to look in steady splendour on the toiling of our kind?
Heart! but this were something nobler than the poet ever felt
When the fought-for happy laurel clasp'd his forehead like a belt;
When the liquid fire of genius, rainbow colour'd, flash'd and glow'd

All its mighty beams above him with the splendour of a god,
Wider in its stretch and grandeur than the brain could ever dream
To look down upon our fellows from some planet's blinding gleam,
Watching with seraphic vision, grasping with delighted soul,
All the goals to which they hurry as the moments shake and roll,
Linking with an unseen quickness vigour to the tasks they do,
Touching each with fresher impulse as a nobler comes in view.
Then when triumph crowns their striving, start to hear the heaven sublime
Fill its azure arch with plaudits echoing from the throat of time,
And to hear the poets singing far above the rush of feet
Epithalamiums of madness when the links of success meet.
This is frenzy, and the overstretching of unhealthy strings,
Let us touch a chord that trembles to the breath of higher things.
Rash in him who sings unworthy, looking not within his heart
For the counsel that should guide him to the honours of his art.
"Sing you thus?" I hear you question, and I answer you again,
I but fit me to that measure chance flings blindly down on men,
Which requires nor heart nor passion, but the will that makes a voice—
Mighty poets sing by impulse, and the lesser but by choice.
"Yet you claim the meed of poet?" and I answer firm and strong,
Count me only as a poet, Brothers, while I sing this song.

Arm to arm, and let the metals into proper range be thrown,
Let us shape the iron pathway for the monster coming on.
What though we be feeble puppets with a little vigour crown'd,
Yet this task is ours, to fence his footsteps into proper bound;
Therefore guide him well, nor tamper with the thread that leads his powers,
Since the splendour of his mission flings a dignity on ours.

As the silent sage at midnight shapes his cunning thoughts to smooth
Pathways through the world's wild jungles for the steady tramp of truth;
As the pioneer that fells the sounding forest tree by tree,
With a mighty thought that trembles to the settlement to be;
As the sentinel who slowly paces as the night hours fly,
With the lives of sleeping thousands hanging on his watchful eye;
As upon the field of Sempach in the bleeding Switzer's breast
Freedom found her purple dwelling, giving to a nation rest;
As the coral insect toiling in the ocean's mighty vast
Rears a giant's labour upward through the swaying surge at last;
So the specks that dot existence, seeming blind and aimless still,
Knit in one, are levers waiting for the touch of thought and will.
Thus are we but toiling units, rough at heart and brown in face,
Noble only being useful, helpful in a humble place;
Filling up the ruts existence furrows with his heavy wain,
That the richer hearts behind may start and sow the fruitful grain;
For we clothe with rougher muscle circles of a mighty whole,
Moving at the touch of fellows with a greater breadth of soul.
But I crave not higher mission than to shape the ends they think,

Deeming I am all but godlike in the holding of a link.
And this link for ever widens, as their restless spirits teach,
Till it forms a chain of union ringing from the heart of each;
Break it and a gap arises never seen until it broke,
As the wires, when cut, are traitors to the sentence-breathing shock;
Heedless of such bond of union grapple we with erring mind,
Feeling not the mighty impulse streaming from our greater kind,
Which, even as the spreading glory waiting on the dying sun,
Shoots along this link that binds us till we feel ourselves as one;
And we grow into their triumph as their works rise up sublime,
Like a book that lies before you glowing with some poet's rhyme;
And the spirit of the minstrel, leaping distance, shoots along,
With a monarch's footsteps marching through the pathways of his song.

Thus the mighty who have labour'd in the ages sunk behind
Knit their spirit to that purpose which they left among their kind;
And forever as the groaning Ages trample under foot
Hydras born of sleeping Wisdom when it pleased her to be mute;
And wherever slow Improvement wanders with a laggard's pace—
Like the Cynic with his lantern roaming in the marketplace
There their power of brain is busy, bringing with its potent rod
Genii from all points of heaven, sets them working with a nod,
In the whirl and sweep of traffic, in the long and restless street,
Multitudinous with its echoes from a thousand feet;
In the clash and clang of hammers, in the anvil's busy sound,
In the belt that like a serpent whirls in hot pursuit around;
In the crash of tooth and pinion slowly forming linkèd rounds;
In the mighty beam that labours, like a Hercules in bounds;
In the slightest puff of steam that specks the ocean far away;
In the sail that dips its shadow far within the lucent bay;
In the furnace darting upward lurid gleams to greet the skies,
Till they start at such a welcome with a flush of red surprise;
In whatever rises up for myriad use with loud acclaim;
In whatever sets for Progress stepping-stones to reach her aim.
But it hath a deeper meaning, and a greater strength and skill,
In the clanking of the rail, and in the engine's thunder still;
For the might of what our fellows can with cunning fingers frame
Moves with him as on he flashes in great bursts of smoke and flame.
Lo, at times as on he strides a quick and glowing frenzy steals
From his sinews swift as light, and from the roar and rush of wheels,
Quick as when the far-off mountains shake themselves from summer mist,
Or the virtue to the woman when she touch'd the hem of Christ—
Filling all the soul within me with a wonder at my kind,
And the nerve and battle onward of this ever-restless mind.
In such fits and heats I wander half a step before the years,
Taking to myself the vision forethought sets apart for seers;
And I see a healthier colour, promise of a Titan's prime,
And a mightier sinew working on the naked arm of Time;

And behind him roars nor cannon, nor the champ of fretting steed,
But the nations leaning forward ready for the swordless deed.
But he waves them back and questions, "Am not I the thought and type
That shall shake the perfect blossom, knowing when the seed is ripe?
Am I not the unseen symbol giving every moment birth,
Breathing with a finger resting on the iron pulse of earth,
Waiting till I feel a calmer action in the glowing vein,
And a wider stretch of bosom ere I stoop to sow the grain?"
This he whispers, and forever as he shakes his restless wings
Silent sands within his hour-glass slip away like earthly things.
But the cycles hid behind him, peering from their shadows still,
Wear upon their brow a purpose which they tremble to fulfil;
Then, for songs to hail their coming, lyrics from some burning heart
Beating with the perfect mission, glowing with the given art.
Higher task is not for poets than to touch with sounding chords
Gleaming Memnons of advance, and shape their whispers into words.
This the task for which the laurel glitters, as upon the thorn
Woven webs of silky slightness swaying in the flush of morn.
Let him take such wreath unblushing, knowing that it is his right,
But his inspiration only as he feels his given might.
Then, when round his brow its coolness circles with inspiring clasp,
Let his thoughts take deeper music, wider range, and higher grasp;
Let him sing the better yearning running through our noble strife,
As from bough to bough the juices creeping start the buds to life;
And the promise growing fuller with the rounding of each year—
O, the future is a giant. We have but his shadow here!

What though Science fills her nectar lavishly in golden cups,
And the earth like a Bacchante all unwitting reels and sups;
She is yet a village maiden, Nature touching not her life,
Girt in dreams of busy childhood, knowing not the aim of wife;
Wearing simple vesture loose in fold that opens to disclose
Breasts that nurse a wish to blossom like the twin buds of a rose,
Then what wonders will they suckle when the juices in her blood
Slowly swell their balmy outline to the round of womanhood:
Like the gods that from Olympus stole into the arms of earth,
Made their nature as a mortal's, and a monster was the birth;
So the thought and might of doing, slipping into her embrace;
Shall be fruitful; and a wonder help the labour of our race.
But from him of double semblance shall she keep the wish'd-for prize,
Heeding not the shallow purpose peering out from narrow eyes;
Only he who toils and battles with an earnest broad desire
Shall receive her fruitful favours, and our fellows shall be higher—
Higher in the nobler feelings, in the wider aims that come,
Pledging all their good to mankind, ever potent, ever dumb.
They shall ride, like one in armour, through the wastes and fens of life,
Giving fight wherever error rears a lance and shield for strife.
They shall usher in the primal order of a happy earth,

Working with their cunning only that a Good may be the birth.

This shall Science do as earnest of her firm and matron prime,
When her passion fruits are growing strong in limb to wrestle time;
They shall watch her slightest motion as she lifts her magic wand,
Rush like Ariels at her sign, and roll the earth into her hand.
Who are they that curb their vision, lifting up with finger tips
Colour'd glass and watch her, crying, that she reels into eclipse?
Narrow hearts that will not widen, souls that in their shells of clay
Flicker up like feeble tapers, but to pass in smoke away;
Prophets that should walk this earth with all their evil croakings wrung
As the shadows swept by Dante in the hell he made and sung;
Ghostly faces looking backward through the shadows thick and vast,
Like Remorse upon a deathbed writhing round to view the past.
Such should be their doom who torture Wisdom into selfish deeds,
Deeming that the earth should wither to give space to sow their creeds.
This were faith in scope and keeping with the brute's within his den;
Let them give their creeds to idiots, but the world to toiling men:
What is all this flash of triumph, from our very footsteps brought,
But the promise of a brighter lying yet unknown to thought—
Brighter in the strength to usher in the many varied use,
As a single bud foreruns a thousand forming the juice.
Yet we grow apace and prosper: All that bath a strength and nerve
Is, like Samson taken captive, made to bow the knee and serve;
And we peer with deepest cunning into seeming useless things,
Train them to a little method, and a miracle upsprings.
Lo, the motion of a finger trifling with a simple wire
Shakes the nations into whispers ere a moment can expire;
And a slight and simple needle shaking in its paltry case
Turns the boundless stretch of ocean to a fearless dwelling-place.
Thus we overleap those wonders kept by ever niggard Time,
Heirlooms of dead worlds behind him ere a blight fell on their prime;
Ah, if they could look upon us from the gloom and dust of years,
Feel our mighty grasp and purpose as the goal we strive for nears;
See the very germ, yet hidden when they pass'd in death away,
Growing into perfect blossom with their fellows yet in clay—
Think you would they turn in wonder to the calm of their abodes,
Blush at all their strength, and worship those who toil'd below as gods?
This is but a wilder fancy creeping through our rugged song;
Yet a burst of rhythmic madness cannot do our fellows wrong,
For in them is nerve and action, will to do and will to dare,
And the demons of their magic work their wonders everywhere.
Hearken! as the world rolls onward with a slow and toiling sound,
All their voices swell and mingle in triumphal hymns around.
Come they from the dash of paddles urging through the spray and foam,
Freights of earnest bosoms outward, freights of smiling faces home;
From the lunge of pistons working scant of room to breathe and pant,
Yet like slaves do all the feats their ever-cunning masters want ;

From the whirring of the spindle in the hot and dusty room,
From the mazes of the wheel, and from the complicated loom,
From the furnace belching outward molten forms at their desire,
Like Enceladus upspringing through his hill of smoke and fire:
Mighty sounds are these, but mightier rush with everlasting hail
From the thunder of the engine and the clanking of the rail.
Ah! the monster that shall mould and make the coming cycles strong—
Shame on me that could desert the inspiration of my song!
So, another pæan, Brothers, ere the fancy sinks away,
Ere we take the voiceless measure ranging through our toiling day.

Arm to arm, and lay the metals, glowing with but one desire—
To do honour to the mightiest of the worshippers of fire.
All the great in early fable, from the mighty Anakim
To each thew'd and swarthy Cyclops, are as nothing unto him.
Yet he seeks our aid and mutters, shaking in his sudden wrath—
Give me but a hand to guide me, give me but a fitting path:
And he snorts and shrieks in triumph as at every bound and rasp,
Like twin threads laid out in distance, all the iron meets his grasp.
Dare we, then, as unto mortals, whisper fear and death to him,
When such breadth of strength like lightning flashes through his heart and limb;
When, within his throbbing bosom, bound with glowing links of fire,
Lies his wildest being panting with the thoughts that cannot tire;
And they hiss, and leap, and flicker, licking up with fiery breath
Strength to feed his sinews working like the flash of swords beneath?
I rise from out my weakness as he flares along my view,
And I deem that I am mighty in the labour others do;
For the Frankensteins who made him part by part and limb by limb
Had the same soul beating in them as my own at seeing him.

Arm to arm, then, lay the metals, let him roll along the rods,
Like Prometheus through the heavens rushing from the angry gods.
Lo! I look into the ages that in spirit we may see
When the hand of death hath stripp'd us from this warp of action free,
And I see this monster stretching his untiring sinews still,
Keeping all his strength, but blindly giving unto men his will;
And they—Lilliputs in muscle, he not deeming them as such,—
Urge his ringing footsteps onward with a paltry fingertouch;
And they link him unto wonders, and their triumphs still increase
Till some awe-struck fellow whispers, "It were time for us to cease."
But they turn and shout an answer, high rebuke in all its tone,
"Shame! and have another planet growing mightier than our own!
Out on such a craven's whisper, all unworthy of our powers,
And this monster toiling with us, making all his being ours.
Forward, then, and let us fashion wider space for his career,
Till the old earth reels and staggers as his sounding footsteps near."
Then they turn to all their labour, shaping as their thought will speak
Pathways into which he glides with iron clutch and madden'd shriek;

And forever as their success brings a wilder aim in view,
Flashes out by fits a wonder at the miracles they do.
Said we not the future's shadow only falls upon us here
As a cloud's upon a hill when all the rest is shining clear?
But to them, our larger fellows of the ages yet to be,
He shall rise, as gods are statured, huge of limb, and broad, and free;
And in frenzy they shall hail him, bring their trophies to his feet,
Then rush on in throngs, and strive to make their wondrous gains complete:
While through all their fret and hurry he, the monster of our song,
Like a wild earth-bound Immortal shall in thunder flash along,
Clasping all things in his vigour, as a serpent flings his coil,
Labour's mightiest Epic rolling through the panting heart of Toil.

BLOOD ON THE WHEEL

"Bless her dear little heart!" said my mate, and he pointed out to me,
Fifty yards to the right, in the darkness, a light burning steady and clear.
"That's her signal in answer to me, when I whistle, to let me see
She is at her place by the window the time I am passing here."

I turn'd to look at the light, and I saw the tear on his cheek—
He was tender of heart, and I knew that his love was lasting and strong—
But he dash'd it off with his hand, and I did not think fit to speak,
But look'd right ahead through the dark, as we clank'd and thunder'd along.

They had been at the school, the two, and had run, like a single life,
Through the mazes of childhood up to the sweeter and firmer prime,
And often he told me, smiling, how he promised to make her his wife,
In the rambles they had for nuts in the woods in the golden autumn time.

"I must make," he would add, "that promise good in the course of a month or two;
And then, when I have her safe and sound in a nook of the busy town,
No use of us whistling then, Joe, lad, as now we incline to do,
For a wave of her hand, or an answering light, as we thunder up and down."

Well, the marriage was settled at last, and I was to stand by his side,
Take a part in the happy rite, and pull from his hand the glove;
And still as we joked between ourselves, he would say in his manly pride,
That the very ring of the engine-wheels had something in them of love.

At length we had just one run to make before the bridal took place,
And it happen'd to be in the night, yet merry in heart we went on;
But long ere he came to the house, he was turning each moment his face
To catch the light by the window, placed as a beacon for him alone.

"Now then, Joe," he said, with his hand on my arm, "keep a steady look out ahead;

While I whistle for the last time;" and he whistled sharply and clear;
But no light rose up at the sound; and he look'd with something like dread
On the white-wash'd walls of the cot, through the gloom looking dull, and misty, and drear.

But lo! as he turn'd to whistle again, there rose on the night a scream,
And I rush'd to the side in time to catch the flutter of something white;
Then a hitch through the engine ran like a thrill, and in haste he shut off the steam,
While, turning, we look'd at each other, our hearts beating wild with affright.

The station was half a mile ahead, but an age seem'd to pass away
Ere we came to a stand, and my mate, as a drunken man will reel,
Rush'd on to the front with his lamp, but to bend and come back and say,
In a whisper faint with its terror—"Joe, come and look at this blood on the wheel."

Great heaven! a thought went through my heart like the sudden stab of a knife,
While the same dread thought seem'd to settle on him and palsy his heart and mind,
For he went up the line with the haste of one who is rushing to save a life,
And with the dread shadow of what was to be I follow'd closely behind.

What came next is indistinct, like the mist on the mountain side—
Gleam of lights and awe-struck faces, but one thing can never grow dim:
My mate, kneeling down in his grief like a child by the side of his mangled bride,
Kill'd, with the letter still in her hand she had wish'd to send to him.

Some little token was in it, perhaps to tell of her love and her truth,
Some little love-errand to do ere the happy bridal drew nigh;
So in haste she had taken the line, but to find, in the flush of her fair sweet youth,
The terrible death that could only be seen with a horror in heart and eye.

Speak not of human sorrow—it cannot be spoken in words;
Let us veil it as God veil'd His at the sight of His Son on the cross.
For who can reach to the height or the depth of those infinite yearning chords
Whose tones reach the very centre of heaven when swept by the fingers of loss?

She sleeps by the little ivied church in which she had bow'd to pray—
Another grave close by the side of hers, for he died of a broken heart,
Wither'd and shrunk from that awful night like the autumn leaves in decay,
And the two were together that death at first had shaken so roughly apart.

But still, when I drive through the dark, and that night comes back to my mind,
I can hear the shriek take the air, and beneath me fancy I feel
The engine shake and hitch on the rail, while a hollow voice from behind
Cries out, till I leap on the footplate, "Joe, come and look at this blood on the wheel!"

A SONG FOR MY FELLOWS

My brothers, in this great world of ours
Our hearts have need to be strong,
And have in them, like shady nooks in a wood,
A shelter for stirring song.
So this snatch of wisdom from Goethe in mine
Is for ever speaking to me,
In the battle of life, from birth unto death
"Thou must hammer or anvil be."

Hammer or anvil, so runs the rhyme,
To beat or be beaten upon—
Whether you stand in the first of the ranks,
Or be left in the rear alone.
But shame on that coward who, faint in his heart,
Would wish to slink from the fray,
Or could bend himself to each turn of the fight,
As a potter might fashion his clay.

Other way must this daily battle be fought,
With no craven heart in the breast,
But keeping keen eye on the colours ahead,
And shoulder and pace with the rest.
The bravest of all the fighters is he
Who, whatever chance may betide,
Can turn and fashion some battle-word
For his fellows on either side.

Then, brothers, let us rise up from our fears,
No anvils are we, but men
Who can wield the sledge-hammer, like mystic Thor,
For the daily battle again.
Let us strike, with an arm to the shoulder bare,
That the sinews may play in their might:
Let us strike for the manhood we feel within
And then we strike for the right.

What truth in the fable we have from the Greek
(A fable is truth at white heat)
Of Hercules smiting the heads off the beast,
Till the monster lay dead at his feet.
It is still in this planet, wherever he tread,
God's own given mission to man,
That he watch for error uprearing her head
And strike wherever he can.

Then seize the sledge-hammer of mighty life,
Let the clanging blows resound;
He strikes the swiftest and surest of all

Who stands on no vantage-ground.
Let this earth of ours, then, from end to end,
Be the anvil steady and strong
Whereon we beat, in the sight of the gods,
The hundred heads of wrong.

What though others around thee turn from the fight
And chatter, a six-feet ape,
Heed them not, for they, too, stand on God's own earth,
But keep true to thyself and thy shape.
Life is earnest only to earnest men,
Sings the high pure Schiller, and so
Let them fashion the blocks of their own rough lives
To the models they worship below.

But he who can feel lying warm at his heart
The higher nature of man,
And can widen the link between us and the brute,
Let him boldly step to the van.
We will follow him on like a leader of old,
And echo his battle cry;
Make way for men that will work like men,
Or, failing, man-like will die.

Yes—the fight will be long, and the heart will droop,
For the ill will seem to win;
But look through the smoke to the goal ahead,
And fall back on the strength within.
Each point that you gain is a step in your life
To lift you nearer the throng
Who have fought and conquer'd, or hero-like died,
With their hands at the throat of some wrong.

Then, brothers, bring into this world's wide field
Firm heart and sure foot for the strife:
No anvils are we for each fool to beat out
His ape-like system of life.
We strive for a higher standard than his,
As we echo our battle cry
Here are men who will work at the tasks of men
Or, failing, man-like will die!"

THE ENGINE

Hurrah! for the mighty engine,
As he bounds along his track:

Hurrah, for the life that is in him,
And his breath so thick and black.
And hurrah for our fellows, who in their need
Could fashion a thing like him—
With a heart of fire, and a soul of steel,
And a Samson in every limb.

Ho! stand from that narrow path of his,
Lest his gleaming muscles smite,
Like the flaming sword the archangel drew
When Eden lay wrapp'd in night;
For he cares, not he, for a paltry life
As he rushes along to the goal,
It but costs him a shake of his iron limb,
And a shriek from his mighty soul.

Yet I glory to think that I help to keep
His footsteps a little in place,
And he thunders his thanks as he rushes on
In the lightning speed of his race;
And I think that he knows when he looks at me,
That, though made of clay as I stand,
I could make him as weak as a three hours' child
With a paltry twitch of my hand.

But I trust in his strength, and he trusts in me,
Though made but of brittle clay,
While he is bound up in the toughest of steel,
That tires not night or day;
But for ever flashes, and stretches, and strives,
While he shrieks in his smoky glee—
Hurrah for the puppets that, lost in their thoughts,
Could rub the lamp for me!

O that some Roman—when Rome was great—
Some quick, light Greek or two—
Could come from their graves for one half-hour
To see what my fellows can do;
I would take them with me on this world's wild steed,
And give him a little rein;
Then rush with his clanking hoofs through space,
With a wreath of smoke for his mane.

I would say to them as they shook in their fear,
"Now what is your paltry book,
Or the Phidian touch of the chisel's point,
That can make the marble look,
To this monster of ours, that for ages lay

In the depths of the dreaming earth,
Till we brought him out with a cheer and a shout,
And hammer'd him into birth?"

Clank, clank went the hammer in dusty shops,
The forge-flare went to the sky,
While still, like the monster of Frankenstein's,
This great wild being was nigh;
Till at length he rose up in his sinew and strength,
And our fellows could see with pride
Their grimy brows and their bare, slight arms,
In the depths of his glancing side.

Then there rose to their lips a dread question of fear
"Who has in him the nerve to start
In this mass a soul that will shake and roll
A river of life to his heart?"
Then a pigmy by jerks went up his side,
Flung a globe of fire in his breast,
And cities leapt nearer by hundreds of miles
At the first wild snort from his chest.

Then away he rush'd to his mission of toil,
Wherever lay guiding rods,
And the work he could do at each throb of his pulse
Flung a blush on the face of the gods.
And Atlas himself, when he felt his weight,
Bent lower his quaking limb.
Then shook himself free from this earth, and left
The grand old planet to him.

But well can he bear it, this Titan of toil,
When his pathway yields to his tread;
And the vigour within him flares up to its height,
Till the smoke of his breath grows red;
Then he shrieks in delight, as an athlete might,
When he reaches his wild desire,
And from head to heel, through each muscle of steel,
Runs the cunning and clasp of the fire.

Or, see how he tosses aside the night,
And roars in his thirsty wrath,
While his one great eye gleams white with rage
At the darkness that muffles his path;
And lo! as the pent-up flame of his heart
Flashes out from behind its bars,
It gleams like a bolt flung from heaven, and rears
A ladder of light to the stars.

Talk of the sea flung back in its wrath
By a line of unyielding stone,
Or the slender clutch of a thread-like bridge,
That knits two valleys in one!
Talk of your miracle-working wires,
And their world-embracing force,
But himmel! give me the bits of steel
In the mouth of the thunder-horse!

Ay, give me the beat of his fire-fed breast,
And the shake of his giant frame,
And the sinews that work like the shoulders of Jove
When he launches a bolt of flame;
And give me that Lilliput rider of his,
Stout and wiry and grim,
Who can vault on his back as he puffs his pipe,
And whisk the breath from him.

Then hurrah for our mighty engine, boys;
He may roar and fume along
For a hundred years ere a poet arise
To shrine him in worthy song;
Yet if one with the touch of the gods on his lips,
And his heart beating wildly and quick,
Should rush into song at this demon of ours,
Let him sing, too, the shovel and pick.

CITY AND VILLAGE

Once again within the city, 'mid its multitudinous din,
Stand I, while, as sinks a leaf when left by the uncertain wind,
So the daily village quiet, and the calm I had within,
Shrinks before the magic contact of the ever-shaping mind.

In the village life is sluggish, waking up but for a space,
As the engines shriek and whistle down by hill and wooded glen;
But here a mightier striving stamps itself upon my race—
Here are all the active ages, and the tramp of busy men.

Then away with daily labour, thoughts of books or weary rhyme,
Let me plunge into this whirlpool rolling on in mad unrest—
Let me, Faust-like, have the weal of men in all the coming time,
That its triumph may strike vigour through the soul within my breast.

Hush! we spoke not of the sorrow that upon their joys will peer,
As the huge unshapen monster glared in on pale Frankenstein,
Edging life's uncertain smile with all the drapery of a tear,
And placing in the cup the drop that dulls and drugs the wine.

But heed not this, and think that, in the rolling on of years,
The slow whirlpool of sure change will lift this life still higher up,
Till it leave behind its apehood, and its daily load of fears,
And drink existence gladly as if angels held the cup.

Far apocalyptic touches that unveil the years to be,
Show this in ecstatic glimpses, as when mists upon a hill
Lift their trailing arms of whiteness, till, as in a dream, we see
A summer gush of glory lying hid behind them still.

Is the pencil of broad Hogarth still to keep its biting truth,
And for ever flash its satire on the world's sweat-blinded sight?
Are we still to stumble onward on a pathway all unsmooth,
Like a Cyclops in his cavern smitten with the loss of light?

Ay, the time will come, my brothers, though it lies behind far hope,
Yet faint flashes rise up from it, like the northern lights we see;
Then, while all the ages come to widen out the mighty scope,
Let us lap ourselves in dreams of what our fellow-men will be.

Look not back with idle murmur lying fretting on thy lips,
That which lies behind is but the crude world's shadow in dull light;
Look thou forward where the sunshine from a kindlier heaven slips,
Cheering on thy kind to wider vantage-grounds for truth and right.

The far ages bristling upward, waiting for their unborn men,
Have in them the golden blossom of the seed we sow in fear;
Wider growths of thought and ripeness, nobler tasks for brain and pen,
Fuller brotherhood in all that perfects us to manhood here.

Heart! to see our future fellows standing on our present gain,
Which we wrench'd from the stern centuries, and Samson-like made ours,
Shaping, with a larger forethought and a finer grasp of brain,
Pathways to the purer use of life and all our human powers.

Theirs shall be our slow improvement rising up to perfect bloom,
Through the centuries niggard of it, like the aloe with its bud;
It shall bring new modes of thinking that shall all the old entomb,
Building up a higher channel for the rushing on of good.

For our fellows striving onward, though they wear the stain of toil,
Ever yearn to shape out goals to which their better natures tend;
And their good within shoots upward, like a plant within the soil,

To the higher, grander freedom, to the nobler godlike end.

Then let change come striking outward, with soft touch or sudden shock,
Let the years glide by, if we can feel that in the lapse of time,
As a leaping mountain torrent through decades can smooth the rock,
We are growing better, wiser, surer of the foot to climb.

For the struggle in the climbing will be hard and ill to bear;
Each one, like the souls in Dante, wearing cloaks and hoods of lead;
But for ever as we struggle, with half breath to breathe a prayer,
From above we hear the echo of another brother's tread.

For the selfless souls amongst us, hearted with the heart of Christ,
Ever turn and beckon onward that their strength may be our own;
And we hear their potent watchwords, which, if we could still resist,
It were shame upon our foreheads burning to the very bone.

All their lives and thoughts are with us, and the strong world's future weal
Will be shaped by what they fought for, though it may be ere it form
(For it will not take their semblance as soft wax takes on the seal),
Cycles may rise up, and set in cloudless calm or sudden storm.

But it will be: higher comfort as we labour scarce can be;
Mists may rise and wrap it from us, but the mighty darting sun
Will strike heat throughout the shadows till like phantom shapes they flee,
Leaving all the good we strove for, and the better laurels won.

Thanks, then, toiling, restless city, that my heart should leap and fill
With such thoughts to help me onward in my own rough life and toil,
That I see through all this hurry one ennobling purpose still;
Dim as yet, but growing brighter, like the mists that leave the soil.

And that purpose still turns brighter at the touch on either hand
Of my fellow-kind who, with me, hold the same high hope of this,
Each one sets it to that music reaching him where he may stand;
But it still keeps ring and measure to the far-off coming bliss.

Teach, then, poet, prophet, priest, with hands stretch'd out to that desire;
Ring it forth to toiling men, and waft it over land and sea,
As the rugged Hebrew prophet, while his eyeballs swam in fire,
Sent down through his vatic brotherhood the Christ that was to be.

Far behind me lies the city, with its ebb and flow of men,
But the thoughts that came within it are for ever in my breast;
And they leap up as the engines thunder down by hill and glen,
Or in my walks at night-time when the village is at rest.

"More coal, Bill," he said, and he held his watch to the light of the glowing fire;
"We are now an hour and a half behind time, and I know that my four months' wife
Will be waiting for me at the doorway just now, with never a wish to tire;
But she soon will get used to this sort of thing in an engine-driver's life."

He open'd the furnace door as he spoke, while I, turning with shovel in hand,
Knock'd the fuel into the greedy flame, that was tossing and writhing about,
Leaping up from its prison, as if in a wrath it had not the power to command,
Shooting narrow pathways of sudden light through the inky darkness without.

Then I turn'd to my place, and as onward we clank'd I sang to myself a snatch
Of a song, to keep time to the grinding wheel (my voice was as rough as its own);
While Harry cried over, from time to time, as he stole a look at his watch,
"Making up for our little delays now, Bill, we shall soon catch the lights of the town:'

A steady fellow was Harry, my mate, with a temper like that of a child;
Loved by all on the line.— "Keeps time like Harry," the guards used to say.
What a marriage was that of his when it came, and how we stokers went wild
To deck our engines with ivy and flowers in honour of such a day.

A nice happy maiden he got for a wife, but a little timid, poor thing—
Never could rest when her husband was late, our "pitchins" were getting so rife;
And this would make Harry cry over to me, as we thunder'd with rush and swing,
"Always like to run sharp to time for the sake of my little wife."

We were now dashing on at a headlong speed, like the sweep of a winter wind,
When a head-light in front made me step to his side and cry, with my mouth to his ear—
"Joe Smith coming on with the midnight goods—he, too, is an hour behind;
He should have been safe through Hinchley cutting, instead of passing us here."

On came the train; but ere we had reach'd in passing the middle part,
A heavy beam in one of the trucks, that had jolted loose from its place,
Crash'd through the storm-board, swift as a bolt, striking Harry full in the heart,
And sent him into the tender with death lying white on his manly face.

With a cry of horror I knelt by his side, and, lifting a little his head,
I saw his lips move as if wishing to speak, but the words were lost in a moan.
"Harry!" He open'd his eyes for a moment, then lifting his finger, said
"O Bill, my wife—behind time;" and I was left on the engine alone.

My God! what a journey was that through the night, with the pall-like darkness before,
And behind the dead form of my mate muffled up, looking ghastly, rigid, and dumb;
And ever on either side as I turn'd, a face at a half-shut door
Peering into the street, to listen the sound of footsteps that never would come.

How that frail slight wife bore the terrible death of the one she had loved so well

I know not; the horror of that one night with the dead was enough to bear;
And the guardsmen who bore their sad burden home, had not language left them to tell
Of the awful depths to which sorrow will reach when led by a woman's despair.

Ah! years have gone by since then, but still when I hear the guards say, "Behind time,"
Like a flash I go back to that hour in the night, mark'd red in my life's return sheet,
And again in my terror I kneel by Harry, struck down in his manly prime,
While his four months' wife stood waiting to hear the wish'd-for sound of his feet.

THE FIRST-FOOT

Bright the firelight touch'd his portrait hanging on our humble wall,
But a sweeter light was in us, with a deeper, purer glow—
He was coming home, our darling—fair and frank, and broad and tall
First-foot on our simple threshold, cover'd with the New Year's snow.

"Twelve o'clock will strike, dear wife, before the train comes in to-night,"
Said my husband at the doorway, he, too, glad at heart and gay;
And he turn'd a step to meet me as I whisper'd, soft and light,
"Let him enter first," and, smiling at my words, he went away.

Then I turn'd, my own heart bursting at the joy about to come,
Drew the chair a little nearer to the glowing evening fire;
Heard in freaks of my own fancy all the laughter and the hum
Of a well-known voice that whisper'd ever at my least desire.

Fondly to myself I pictured all his much-prized honours won,
Earnest of the future harvests that the years would open up;
Caught a hundred whispers rising with this burden still, "our son;"
O! a mother's joy has not one drop of gall within the cup.

Then I went, and by the window watch'd with eager gazing eye
All the distant railway lights that slowly came in sight to me;
Question'd to myself, "Now, which of these far lights is bringing nigh
Our first-foot for the New Year that in one little hour will be?"

But a deep chill, like a viper's touch, crept through me as I stood,
Bringing hand-in-hand a terror, as behind the farthest light
Rose another in the darkness, that like one great splash of blood,
Gleam'd like a murder seen of God within the folds of night.

Rooted to the place I stood, and watch'd its steady, fiery gleam,
All the pulses in my being beating as in act to fail;
And my heart sank down within me, like a stone flung in the stream,
As behind it rose an engine's whistle with a ghostly wail.

For at that drear whistle all the years broke from their rusty bands,
Each one teeming with its fatal slip that happen'd in a breath—
How a traitor wheel, or pointsman's hasty clutch of faithless hands,
Scatter'd broadcast human lives to grace the silent feast of death.

Ah! what battles hope had all that weary hour with countless fears;
What deep, silent prayers rose upward that the lips still fail'd to speak;
What deep pain within the bosom, with its load of unwept tears,
That would not give one kindly drop to soften brow or cheek.

Came the hour at last, and striking, each stroke sounded like a knell,
Bodeful of some fate—but, hark! a sound of footsteps at the gate,
And my tears burst from their prison, and rose upward like a well,
At the coming joy about to crown my long and weary wait.

Then I heard the sound of whispers faint, as if in awe suppress'd,
And with all my wild, deep dread within, I open'd up the door—
Saw a burden in strange arms, and in their silence found the rest
O my God! first-foot in heaven! and for days I knew no more.

Slowly dawn'd the truth upon me, as my life came back again—
How a signal, clear a moment to the engine-driver's eye,
Brought him on with ringing rush and crash against and through the train!
And my life's one hope lay mangled in that sudden shock and cry!

Years have pass'd, but still that time brings round the great red light to me;
With it come the solemn footsteps, and the whispers hush'd and low;
And again the door is open'd, while like one struck dumb I see
My darling's blood with that round light upon the ghastly snow.

RID OF HIS ENGINE

The way that it came about was this—
I was stoker for over two years to Bill,
But do as we might something went amiss
With that creaking confounded engine still.

We never ran time, and were always late;
Now a throttle valve would get choked and stop,
Then an axle grow hot as a coal in the grate,
Next a tube would burst, and—into the shop.

How Bill did swear when delays took place;
He would chew till his lips were almost black,
Then say, with an oath, looking into my face—
"I wish I was rid of this engine, Jack."

But she stuck to us still, like one of the Fates,
Snorting and creaking on, until
A sort of proverb grew up with our mates,
"Six hours behind time, like Jack and Bill."

Well, one night on our way through Deepside Moss—
It was then our turn out with the midnight goods—
Bill had sworn at the engine till he was cross,
And was now into one of his quieter moods.

When, just as I lifted up my head
From the furnace-door, there right in front
(I had miss'd the signal standing red),
Was a mineral train that had stopp'd to shunt.

I shut off the steam, and I shook up Bill
"For God's sake look out"—when with one wild roar,
And a crash that is making my ears ring still,
We pitch'd into the train, and I knew no more.

When I came to myself I was down the bank,
Half-a-yard from my head lay a waggon wheel,
With its axle twisted and bent like a crank,
But no hurt was upon me that I could feel.

Then I heard coming downward the sound of speech,
And struggling up to the top, I found
That engine and tender lay piled upon each,
With a fencework of waggons and vans around.

"What a smash!" said the guard, and I ask'd "Where's Bill?"
He turn'd, and the light of his lamp was cast
On a form at my feet, lying stiff and still:
Bill had got rid of his engine at last.

JIM'S WHISTLE

No, the railway wasn't a fitting place
For a man like him, at least one in his case;
But though deaf and dumb, he was quick of the eye,
And was first to warn when a train came nigh.
Why, instead of keeping our eye on Jim,
We came in our turn to be watch'd by him.

Whether it was express going past,

Special, mineral, goods, slow or fast,
It was all the same. Jim could always catch
Up and down line, as if set to watch.
When we heard his cry, short, sharp, and clear,
"Jim's Whistle," we said, and at once stood clear.

Clever workman he was, and handy, too;
Knew at a glance what he had to do;
He was my mate, and 'twas something to see
The finger talk between him and me,
And to hear him laugh to the rest of our mates
When he tried to tickle me over the plates.

At our dinner hour, when we sat at the side
Of the cutting, Jim took a sort of pride
In sitting near me, while his fingers said
All the quaint, strange thoughts that came into his head;
While at each he would laugh, till the rest would say,
"Jim's in one of his talking moods to-day."

But I lost him at last: though my mate for years,
And quick of the eye; I had still my fears,
That Jim would get caught in spite of our pains,
By engine and tender or passing trains.
And it came at last so sudden and quick,
We left in the four-feet shovel and pick.

'Twas in Dixon's cut. Jim had been that day
Full of finger talk in his own swift way,
When, just as we clear'd the down line for a train
That was coming onward with jolt and strain,
Round the curve of the up line, swift as the wind,
Came a passenger train, half-an-hour behind.

A cry from us all and a leap to the side
As the train tore on with its terrible stride;
But where was Jim? We had miss'd his cry—
The whistle that warn'd when a train was nigh.
Alas! in the six-feet, stiff of limb,
With the blood on his face and lips lay—Jim.

I ran to his side and lifted his head,
One look was enough—my mate was dead;
I laid him down in the self-same place,
Then turn'd away with the tears on my face.
"Jim's Whistle," said one, that was all our speech,
As we stood in our grief looking each at each.

And now at my daily work, other mate
Than Jim on the other side of the plate,
I sometimes start with the wish to cry,
"Jim's Whistle, lads, let the train go by."
And often my fingers go up, as if Jim
Were with me, and I were talking to him.

MOVE UPWARD

Ay, in heaven's name, let us move upward still
In this time-changing planet of ours,
And bring to the task what the gods still ask—
The best of our years and our powers.
Let us make this great century, whirling around,
A footstool to lift up the foot,
Whereon we may cry, looking upward to God—
"We are all this way from the brute."

Is the dream of the poet forever to be
Like the myth of the Greek, or at least
The skeleton dress'd up in costliest gold,
And set in the midst of the feast?
Is the double meaning forever to wind
Like the coil of the snake round our speech?
And the Dead Sea fable still utter its truth
As we mimic and chatter to each?

But questions are weapons an infant can lift,
Let us marry the fruitfuller act,
And widen our being to let in the light,
And the strength of the deed-giving fact.
Is it not enough we have come from God?
But since time took his birthright in years,
We have bred with the brute, and our offspring has been
The sucklings of bloodshed and tears.

It were time, then, to burst from the links we have forged
To fetter the soul in the breast,
Though the wrench should bring with it the best of our blood,
And we faint as a pilgrim for rest.
Heart! but each has some task he must close with his life
When he slips from this world's wide plan,
And the highest a man can shape out for himself
Is to move himself upward to man.

Ay, move himself up to that nature of his

Which, though trampled and trod in the dust,
Still shows, as a jewel may gleam through the sand,
The finger of God through its crust.
Let him, then, so alive with miraculous breath,
Make the best of his energies join,
Till he lift himself up in the light of the Christ
To the clear, true ring of the coin.

There be some who squat down by the world's rough path,
As if life were a burden to shirk,
Heeding not the great watchword it thunders to all—
"Up, shoulder to shoulder, and work!"
But sit in their darkness to wince at the truth,
As an owl at the light sits and blinks,
And for ever propound each his question to solve,
Like a nineteenth-century Sphinx.

"Move upward from what?" they demand, with a croak,
And I break in at once and reply
"From the sham that has flung our soul under its heel,
And the words that but wrap up a lie—
From the thought that still grovels and hides in the dust,
As a viper may do, until blind
It springs up to find venom to add to its own,
In the plague-spots seen in our kind."

Ay, battle with this as a fighter strikes out,
When he stands with his back to the wall,
With no help but the strength that is in his right arm,
And the eye that has glances for all.
Shame on us, then, who stand with our face to the front,
And modell'd in God's mighty shape,
If we roughen our soul with the dust of the earth,
To give better foothold for the ape.

God! to look on this manifold, wonderful earth,
As Novalis look'd on men,
And feel the old rev'rence grow upward within
To the pitch of the Hebrews again—
To have the rapt soul and the calm, deep eye
That can look upon all without fear,
And the firm, steady beat of the heart that can feel
When the footsteps of God are anear.

It may be that we may, fighting upward to this,
Grow footsore and faint in the heat,
But the moving oneself up to heights in this life
Spreads no carpeted way for the feet.

Let us think of those grand, true souls who have left
Guiding-posts on each side of the way,
And press ever on with our eyes to the light
They have left as a part of their day.

Ay, in Heaven's name, let us move upward, then,
To the grand, true ring of the man,
Giving to this one task all the best of our years,
And the strength to reach up to the plan.
Let the "Ernst ist das Leben " of Schiller speak on,
Till we seize and place under our foot
The head of the ape, crying upward to God,
"Lo! at last we are free from the brute!"

SONG OF THE ENGINE

In the shake and rush of the engine,
In the full, deep breath of his chest,
In the swift, clear clank of the gleaming crank,
In his soul that is never at rest;
In the spring and ring of the bending rail,
As he thunders and hurtles along,
A strong world's melody fashions itself,
And this smoke-demon calls it his song.

"Hurrah! for my path I devour in my wrath,
As I rush to the cities of men
With a load I lay down like a slave at their feet,
Then turn and come backward again.
Hurrah! for the rush of the yielding air
That gives way to my wild, fierce springs
As I keep to the rail, while my heart seems to burst
In a wild, mad craving for wings.

"I rush by hills where the shepherds are seen
Like a speck as they walk on their side;
I roar through glens and by rocks that shake
As I quicken the speed of my stride.
I glide by woods and by rockbound streams
That hurry and race in their glee,
But swift as they run, with their face to the sun,
They can never keep pace with me.

"I tear through caverns of sudden dark,
Like that in which first I lay,
Ere the cunning of man had alit on a plan

To drag me up to the day.
I rush with a shriek, which is all I can speak,
A wild protest against fear;
But I come to the light with a snort of delight,
And my black breath far in the rear.

"I crash along bridges that span the hills,
And catch at a glimpse below
The roof-thatch'd cot and the low white wall
Lying white in the sun's last glow.
Or it may be the gleam of some dull, broad stream
Creeping slowly onward beneath,
While within its breast for a moment I catch
The shadow and film of my breath.

"I rush over roofs in my madness of flight,
But not like the demon of old;
I leave them unturn'd, for the arches in air
Bear me up, and my feet keep their hold.
At times, too, I catch, when I check my speed,
The long, wide lane of the street,
And hear, 'twixt the snorts of my own fierce breath,
The clamour and hurry of feet.

"Then I snatch a look at the puppets beneath,
But to snort and rush onward again,
With a fear at my heart almost quenching its heat,
For, heavens ! these must be men—
Ay, men, I could bend like the willow, but who,
With a thought that from nothing will shrink,
Have hurl'd me down with their hands on my throat,
And bound me in rivet and link.

"I rush by village, and cottage, and farm;
I thunder sudden and quick
Upon handfuls of men who leap out of my way,
And lean on their shovel or pick.
There is one brown fellow among them who sings
The terrible sweep of my limb;
The fool! dare he mimic this music of mine,
And such pitiful music in him?

"I flare through the night when the stars are bright,
With the lights of the city for mark:
With bound upon bound I shake the ground,
As I feel for the rail in the dark.
And I know that the stars whisper each to each,
As downward they flicker and peer,

'What is this that these fellows have hit on below,
That seems like a meteor from here?'

"For my great eye glistens and gleams in the front,
As if to give light to my tread,
While behind, like the fires of a Vulcan flung out,
Three others glare thirsty and red.
And the flame licking round the fierce life in my heart,
Let loose for a moment, upsprings,
And darts through the whirls of my breath overhead,
Till it makes me a demon with wings.

"I send through the city's wild heart shocks of life,
But to feel them come back like a wave;
I loom broad and swart in wild traffic's rough mart,
I kneel to men like a slave.
I gather from all the four ends of the earth,
What profit and use there may be—
Did the Greek ever dream, in his talk with the gods,
Of a wild beast of burden like me?

"But often my own wild thoughts leap far ahead,
And I question myself with a moan—
'Will I ripen and grow into sinew and limb
With the higher race that comes on?
Or shall I grow white with the hoar of the years
That, falling, cankers and wears—
Turning feeble of limb with the things that benumb,
And steal the vigour from theirs?

"'Were this worthy end for a being like mine,
Begot in the frenzy of thought,
And sent as the type of the soul of this age,
Setting time and distance at nought?
No, death may leap back, like men from my track,
For my iron-girt bosom will beat,
Till the judgment-bolts flung from the right hand of God
Smite the pathway from under my feet.'"

Thus he snorts and sings as he thunders by me,
This wild smoke-demon of ours,
While from end to end the rail quivers and bends
To his thousand Hercules' powers.
And his great breath mixes and whirls with the clouds,
While he whoops as if mad with glee
"Did the Greek ever dream, in his talk with the gods,
Of a black beast of burden like me?"

On the engine in the night-time, with the darkness all around,
And below the iron pulses beating on with mighty sound.
And I stand as one in wonder, till within a flush of pride
Leaps and kindles, and my soul is in the mighty monster's stride.
Then I hear amid the clanking and the tumult of the steel,
Something like a song spring upward from the grinding of the wheel,
Low at first but high and higher, till, as day is wide and free,
Comes the song, and this mad lyric sings the monster unto me:—
"In the glowing of my bosom, in the roar and rush of fire,
Is the strength that makes the distance shrivel in to my desire,
And I roll along in thunder swift as is the lightning fleet—
Let the Frankensteins who made me keep the guiding of my feet,
For I work with them and labour, bearing in my smoky mirth
All the strain and rush of traffic, as an Atlas bears the earth;
Striving with them till my sinews, bending to their mighty load,
Shake and glisten like the muscles on the shoulder of a god.
Shame that I should let such puppets move me at their slightest will—
I, the Cyclops of this darkness, with a forehead flaming still—
I who have within a vigour equal to all fabled power,
And the soul of mad Prometheus, with his cunning for a dower!
But they draw me onward, placing slips of rail beneath my tread,
While my fiery strength within me to a thousand tasks is wed,
So that all my panting being, marvelling at such display,
Questions, as I foam and thunder, 'Who is greater? I or they?'
This I heed not, for their purpose mixing ever with my own,
Keeps the iron will within me pulsing to a proper tone.
Therefore let my mission widen till my shriek of triumph rings,
Ever from the front of progress leading onward human things.
Lo! the ages yet that slumber in the mighty womb of Time,
At their birth shall gather round me, for my strength shall touch its prime.
They shall hail me as their king, and bring round my giant life
All this mad and restless planet, with its myriad forms of strife.
Then a deeper thirst shall stir me, and a wilder vigour cling
To my never-tiring sinews, as my iron footsteps ring.
Puppets of a restless frenzy, they shall work me till the earth
Bears upon her farthest bosom fiery tokens of my birth.
But I make myself a prophet, yet these miracles shall be,
And be sung in lyrics worthy of this iron heart in me.
Therefore thou who standest wondering while I toil and shriek along,
See that all my world-wide mission touch thee into proper song.
Sing the nerve and toil within me, and the vast desires that fret
Till before them all their purpose and their mighty goals are set;
Sing them unto men in music, rough as is my tortured shriek,
When my strength flares up within me, and my mighty soul must speak,

So that I may hear their pæans as I flash and thunder on,
The rough Hercules of Labour, ever potent and alone."

Thus the monster sang, and ever as he sped with flash and glare
All his fiery thoughts went upward, like red stars into the air,
And each throb that shook his being found a ready voice in mine,
Crying—All the soul within him is but as a part of thine;
Then a deeper pride grew in me, and my heart beat higher still,
For I felt myself a part of all his iron strength and will—
Mine the endless grasp of sinew, mine the miracle of mind,
Mine the glory and the triumph of my toiling fellow-kind.
Thus I thought; and through the night time, as the monster clank'd along,
I grew prouder of my labour and my little gift of song.

A SONG OF PROGRESS

Come away from pick and shovel for another day again,
Glide along the veins of iron leading to the city's heart,
Walk its streets and rub a shoulder with my wondrous fellow-men,
Then come back and stand with firmer foot in labour's toiling mart.

Thus I thought as ever onward, through the golden summer day,
Went the engine, all his pathway ringing answers to his tread,
Heard him shriek at every steady arm of red that cross'd his way,
His great nineteenth century watch-cry for the world to move ahead.

Ah! what toil in dark and daylight, aching brain and weary eye,
Waiting for the magic thought to burst its cycled chrysalis,
Till at last, like some Messiah, Science brings her handmaids nigh,
And we stand on stairs of centuries with a mighty thing like this!

He, our wild familiar, tamed to rush where'er we point or speak,
Turning, where his footsteps wander, earth into one mighty mart;
Looming in the midst of traffic, as from out the ranks of Greek
Tower'd the elephant, that terror sent to every Roman's heart.

Lo! at last the toiling city, where the foremost ranks of life
Rush and strive in ceaseless struggle, ebbing but to come again;
And my heart leaps up within me, palpitating for the strife,
In the maelstrom of swart traffic, in the toil and shock of men.

Here is life on either hand that might disturb each idle god—
Drowsy-brain'd, with golden nectar bubbling from Hebean cup:
Life, as if some mighty giant had beneath these streets abode,
And was stretching every muscle in his frenzy to burst up.

Shame on all the later devil's whisper, crying in our ear—
"We are apes of broader forehead, with the miracle of speech;"
Rather nineteenth century men, that have a thought Who sent us here:
Higher faiths are ours, my fellows, low enough for us to reach.

What though I, your feeble helpmate, stand among you all unknown?
Yet each pulse within me, as a hand laid on responsive strings,
Vibrates to each new-shaped purpose rising up within your own,
Ringing forth excelsior pæans for the onward march of things.

Everywhere to bound the vision, the miraculous faith of toil
Rears, as worship, mighty monsters with their hundred arms flung loose;
Miles of vessels throbbing in their haste to fling a liquid coil
Of commerce round the nations kneeling with their proffer'd use.

What a seven-leagued stride from Adam, and the languor of the East,
To this century lapping round us, like a mad and hungry sea,
To the chainless brain that, like the gem, from the dark released,
Fills the earth with triumphs, earnest of the greater yet to be.

Heavens! how the unseen multitudinous coils of serpent thought
Draw this earth within their clasp, till, as upon the father's face,
Where the Deity of pain grew, as the throbbing sculptor wrought,
So her rugged features lighten, lying in their firm embrace.

But I wander from the city. Let me turn again to find
In the waves of human faces rolling past on either side
Links that, strong as bands of iron, draw me onward to my kind,
Till their fellowship shoots through me with electric thrills of pride.

For in them is the sure seed from which the ages yet to be,
Rising up with great broad sickle, shall reap all its golden grain;
Then the kindlier thought and nobler use of manhood shall be free,
And be brighter from the struggle such a sunny height to gain.

This we may not see; yet, brothers, it were something grand to die
But to hear a shout ring upward, through the death-mists thick and vast,
Loud as when a thousand people join their voice in one long cry,
That the world's great fight for brotherhood had clutch'd the palm at last.

It will come: I hear its promise ringing on from street to street
(Shame if we could play for ever at the game of Hoodman-blind):
I can see it; other mark than Cain's upon each brow I meet;
And the engine's whistle shrieks it as the city sinks behind.

Back to honest pick and shovel, and to daily task again—
Back with nobler thoughts within me, all the higher aims to cheer;
Better, too, in having rubb'd a shoulder with my fellow-men,

And the thinking that I help them at my lowly labour here.

THE FIRST BREAK

The first break in our happy household hearth
Was my broad manly son, and far away
He sleeps, while by the churchyard's holy earth
Throb the great engines onward day by day.

Ah me! and as I hear in this strange land
Their whistle from the distant town, I feel
As if I saw him slipping foot and hand,
And lying crush'd beneath the heartless wheel.

Then I live o'er again that awful night,
When to my door the whisper'd message came,
That made my heart leap up with sudden fright,
And all the silence tremble with his name.

A splash of blood fell everywhere I look'd,
Turning my tears to the same purple hue,
While in me rose dread fears my heart rebuked,
As all his vanish'd life rose up to view.

They brought him home, and up the little street
They bore him slowly to his early rest,
Laying the green sod, that of old his feet
Had trod in Sabbath days, upon his breast.

He slept, while in my heart I bore the pain
That still would live at times, until at last
My being's inner depths closed up again,
And gave but little token of the past.

Then came a change. I left that dear old spot
Where boyhood, manhood, all had come to me—
Came here among my sons, but never brought
My heart, for that was still beyond the sea.

Yet that one night before I left, I took
My stand beside his grave, and with hush'd breath,
Raised to the skies a father's silent look,
And took mute farewell of the dust beneath.

Then, turning as beneath some sudden blight,
I stagger'd down the churchyard big with fears,

Went down the street for the last time, the night
Around me hiding all my bitter tears.

I reach'd my lowly home, now cold and dim;
Sat by the hearth, a shadow on my mind,
Thinking how all around me seem'd like him
Whose dust cost such a pang to leave behind.

I sail'd. And now between me and that home
The ocean rolls with never-ceasing moan,
Checking all in me save my dreams, that roam
To bring old faces nearer to my own.

But still, whenever from the distant town
I hear the engine shriek, then far away
I wander to that grave, where up and down,
Close by his rest, they thunder day by day.

IN THE VANGUARD

Into all the onward current and this iron time that feels
Its own way with din and clamour through this century of ours
Come I, while the toiling planet like some stricken monster reels
In an overheat to reach the very climax of its powers.

But the ages, ever watchful of their growing higher need,
Cry—"Before we hail him poet, glowing with the vatic mood,
He must, with his brow turn'd upward, stand like rock upon his creed,
Ours shall be the task to shelter what may spring from where he stood."

Then I answer—"One great creed is mine, but as the blinding sun
Draws the unseen stars in day-time, though we try in vain to see.
So the lesser creeds twine round it, as it towers in height alone;
That one faith is trust in God and Christ and all the great To Be.

All the lesser are the social bands that knit me to my kind,
Farther progress, higher culture, and the touch of purer thought,
Passing on the watchward 'Forward,' to another kindred mind,
Fighting for the broader platform as an earnest fighter ought."

Then the ages pause a moment, all unnoted of the earth,
Speak in earnest; half-heard whispers, then turn slowly round again,
Crying, "If this fellow yearns to battle for the purer birth,
Let him pass and fight it out amid his boasted fellowmen."

So I come, then, brothers, shoulder touching shoulder in the throng;

Shame if I could stand thus feeling all the kindred aims ye bear
With my lips shut, like Ridolpho's, as in Dante's solemn song,
Nor give one single echo to the music leaping there.

If there be in song a hidden, talismanic force and power,
That for ever lifts us upward to the purer life and thought,
It were something but to leave behind, though dying in an hour,
Some stray note of music chording with the great world's as it ought;

Or, to think that in our toiling some quick fragment of that flame
Which from nature ever clasps its coils of living fire round men,
Might be put in words by us and shot, with hundred-tongued acclaim,
From firm heart to heart, until it struck back on our own again.

Ay, to catch in some wild frenzy, as the painter dash'd his brush
'Gainst the passive canvas, mad to grasp the wild wave's mimic foam,
All the thought that, like a Pallas, still unseen will ever rush
From the brain of the wide present to the grander time to come.

So the deep, forecasting poet, glowing with his rhythmic art,
Leans against the broad-based future while his soul in visions dips;
Rising with some mighty lyric, shooting throbs from heart to heart,
Caught when nature fell upon him with her own apocalypse.

But I come not with such lyrics—mine have not the ring and sound
To catch the swift world's straining ear, athirst for nobler things;
Yet my hand and heart are yearning for a power to be unbound,
That my soul may catch some music worthy of the higher strings.

"Lo, he comes," perchance some whisper, "with a thought laid out for wrong,
Little points of poison-blisters, plentiful in modern days;
Lo, he comes with something in him that unwisely takes to song,
Croaking from a dusty railway for a paltry boon of praise!"

Heavens! praise were worthless fruit to pluck and gather in these years,
When the loftier thought must grow, and all the lower, baser aims
That fling roots down, like the banyan, must be torn up with our tears,
That the future may not wear upon its brow a thousand shames. ,

What is all this earth around us but a place to wrestle in,
Foot to foot and hand to hand with all the beasts that must be fought?
Fight it out, and let the still gods turn their thumbs up when we win,
Like the Romans in the circus when their blood ran swift and hot.

Fight with hate and scorn and envy, fight with all that saps the man;
We have grand, true types before us, shame on those who turn and yield!
Better lying dead, to serve as stepping-stones to raise the van,
Than lose all this noble manhood, and return without our shield.

Oh, that some great painter, glowing with the secret of his art,
Would place upon the canvas, when his thought was pure and high,
A dead Spartan, kill'd in fight, that we might catch with soul and heart
The wild energy of purpose not yet quench'd within his eye!

Honour to the great and noble on whatever ground they stand,
If they give us higher stand-points—for such office were they sent;
Honour to them, if we feel the strong grasp of an unseen hand
Leading us to what they fought for by the pathways that they went.

In these days they speak of missions; noblest of them all is this,
That we train our manhood upward, till the grand and fearless thrill,
Which, ere Adam lost his splendour, ran like bands of steel through his,
Lies like fire about our hearts, to keep our purpose earnest still.

For we are not as some preach, with faithless hands that beckon doubt,
Drops of life from godless matter struck by some stray random touch,
When the forces play'd at blind buff, but by God Himself shaped out—
Autographs of Him in flesh, yet all unworthy to be such.

Then we dare not but move upward, though we falter in our tread,
Though we feel around our limbs the paralysing coils of fear;
Lo! afar we hear brave whispers coming from the earnest dead,
As the old heroic voices sung with winds in Ossian's ear.

Up, then, to our life-long fight, and fling the gage of battle down,
Let the ages bear our word of rally onward far and quick;
Nobler usage of this manhood, from the king who wears a crown
Down to ourselves, my brothers, working with the spade and pick!

BILL'S LENGTH

"On to Bill's length," said my mate to me.
Bill was his brother, had charge of the plates
From Horsely's cutting to Whitefield gates,
And the two were as loving as brothers could be.

"On to Bill's length," said my mate again.
"I wonder if he has flung into line
That place by the bridge where we gave him the sign,
The run before last, to go up with his men.

"But here is the bridge." It had suddenly grown
Out of the mist. As we shot below
The arch, we hitch'd, and my mate cried, "Joe,

We must signal to Bill as we journey down."

Up rose the mist, and at last we could see
The signals at Colpey junction clear.
"Take off the brake; we have nothing to fear,
And put out the headlight," said Dick to me.

I went, but my face, as I hurried back,
Made him come to my side with a look of alarm.
"For God's sake," I cried, taking hold of his arm,
"Draw within the distant signals and slack."

Off went the steam, and I hung by the brake;
Two minutes, and we had our train at a stand.
I sprang down the steps, waving Dick with my hand
To keep back for a moment, just for my sake.

I rush'd to the front of the engine, and there,
With a feeling of sickening horror and dread,
Drew out from where it lay fix'd a head,
With the features half-cover'd with blood and hair.

I turn'd, and Dick (I can see him still)
Gave a look of horror and mute appeal,
Then moan'd as he stagger'd against the wheel,
"My God! that's the head of my brother Bill."

Just as he said: Bill had been on the rail,
Ready to make out the day's repair,
And the mist coming down, we had unaware
Run him down, for we always drove fast with the mail.

Dick left the line, and it never was known
Where he went; but often I think of that day,
And still by the bridge I can hear him say,
"We must signal to Bill as we journey down."

THE SPIRIT OF THE TIMES

Come, fling for a moment, my fellows,
The pick and shovel aside,
And rise from the moil of our ten hours' toil
With a heart beating high with pride.
What though our mission can do without thought,
And the music and cunning of rhymes;
Yet shame on that bosom that will not throb

To the spirit and march of the times.

Then, hurrah! for this rough, firm earth of ours,
Like a lion half-roused from his den
She wakes up, and cries, while we whisper in fear,
"Let us hush her to sleep again."
But a voice from the very footstool of God
Cries, "Break her away from her thrall,
That our fellows may toss her from hand to hand,
As a juggler tosses his ball."

Come, then, let us thunder our watchword still,
"Make way for the tools and the man,"
Let the rough hand work what the thought will shape
To its highest miraculous plan—
Till the gods, who loll at the edge of the stars,
Look down as we labour below,
And swear by their nectar these puppets beneath
Know at least how their planet should go.

Fling the span of the bridge o'er the foam of the sea,
Run shafts to the centre of earth,
Wrench the coal from her grasp to the light of the sun,
That the giant of steam may have birth.
Lay the pliant rail on her full broad breast,
That, swift as a lion springs,
The engine may hurtle and roar—the Danton
Of this wondrous new birth of things!

Build the ship into being from stem to stern,
But not with wood as of yore,
But with iron plates that may laugh at the shock
Of the thunder hammer of Thor.
Let the sea swell up in his white-lipp'd wrath,
As the circling paddles fly,
And Neptune himself groan for want of room
Till the iron hulk goes by.

O, fellows, but this is a wondrous age,
When Science with faith in her eyes,
Springs up in her thirst from this planet of ours
To the stars in front of the skies.
And we—we watch her as onward she glides
Leaving wonders behind her track,
Like a huntsman that jerks a hawk from his wrist,
But who will whistle her back?

Ay, who? for at length she has found her strength,

As a tiger's may come at the sup
Of the warm first blood, and his wild fierce mood
Like fire through his frame flashes up;
So she, and we follow as onward she leads
With the flush of pride on her cheek,
And she makes us the greater men, though we work
In the wake of the Roman and Greek.

Shame rest on the bigot that thinks in his heart
She flings a-blight on our creeds,
And darkens the light that we keep to guide
As we rush from the fable to deeds.
Out on such croakers! with one white hand
She lifts her miracle rod
And strikes wherever we wish, while the other
Holds on by the garments of God.

The ages behind look like infants in sleep,
But those that look down on our time
Cry out with a hundred voices in one
To nourish them into prime.
And, God! but we build them up to their strength,
As an eagle will rear her young,
But their giant force, springing up like a source,
Has never yet been sung.

Where shall he come from, the poet, whose fire
Shall place on his wild, rough page
The spirit that lurks and forever works
In the breast of this mighty age?
Is he yet in the cycles that loom before,
Preparing his melody?
Let him come, and roll through my heart and soul
His music before I die.

But now, while we wait for the roll of his words,
Let us work in our growing strength;
For the earth in her cradle, since Adam died,
Is up from her slumber at length.
Ay, up! in the cities that roar and fret
With the toil and the tread of men;
And the sun shall be hurl'd from his course ere she sinks
To her second childhood again!

Then, hurrah! for our higher fellows that work
With this thought and its Titan powers,
And cut through the jungle of creeds and fools
A path for this planet of ours.

And hurrah for this nineteenth century time—
What the future may grow and be!
Ah, God! to burst up from the slumber of death
For one wild moment to see!

ON THE ENGINE AGAIN

Once more on the mighty engine, boys,
With my hand on the driver's arm,
And again at his touch through each fire-leading vein
Throbs a flood of the life-giving charm.
Then away he speeds as a light in the north
Shooting up makes the heavens grow pale;
At my feet the glow and the beat of his heart,
And beneath them the ring of the rail.

Hurrah! how each sweep of his lightning limb
Flashes swifter than that of the last,
While, wild as the flight in a dream of the night,
The distance is galloping past.
On, on, with a madder desire in his breast
For the space that is yet to be run,
Till a dozen slim wires stretching out on my right
Seem to narrow and rush into one.

How my blood flushes up, like wine dash'd in a cup,
At the headlong speed of his race,
While he shrieks in his glee, and looks back at me,
And flings his breath in my face.
Half a world is left in the distance behind,
Yet he never slacks in his stride,
Nor a drop of sweat is seen glancing yet
On the iron girths of his side.

Hurrah! I lean over and pat his neck,
As a rider might that of his horse,
While beat goes my heart like a Cyclops at work,
At this terrible acme of force.
I hear the ring of the rail, and the click
Of the joint, as he roars o'er his track,
And I shriek in my frenzy, "A steed for the gods
Or some Titan Mazeppa to back."

By heaven! but this would have been the one
To have hurl'd with a snort and shriek
From the door of his temple, the battle car

Of the warrior god of the Greek;
Or have led the front of those coursers that rush,
With the dawn like foam on their breast,
And whirl the sun, through a dust of clouds,
To his purple home in the west.

And I think that he fathoms my thoughts, for his form
Seems to wilder energy strung,
And gleams as might that of some serpent when he
Tightens up the last coil that he flung;
Or it may be, in wrath when he looks behind
To leap at the light-shapen elf,
And hurl him beneath the wild rush of his feet,
And take the reins to himself.

I turn, and lo! with a flash and a glare
His breast is thrown open to see,
And I start in affright at the wild, fierce light
That is leaping to clutch at me.
Then I whisper, the bloodless fear on my lip,
As the flame tongues flicker and dance
"God, he too has a fire round his heart, like those kings
In the Eblis hall of romance!"

But this fire within him is the nerve in his limb,
And his pulse's hurry and shock,
As he toils, a man-made Prometheus, bound
To the rail instead of the rock.
The coward, he dare not slip from the line,
That is guiding his feet beneath,
For his soul would burst from him in gushes of flame,
Like a sword drawn in haste from its sheath.

So a trust without doubt in the lines leading out
The sinewy sweep of his length,
Keeps him still to their grasp, though his vigour within
Fain would lift him in frolic of strength.
Ah, me! could I so keep true to my life,
And the good that would fain lead me on,
And turn my breast, like his own great chest,
To the war we must battle alone.

But this thought sinks away as I ask in my fear,
Will he never halt in his speed,
But rush onward and shriek his wild watchword, "Go on,"
Like the Jew in the legend we read?
No! Far in the distance, in front of his goal,
Springs upward a finger of red,

And with a death-rattle of one wild snort
His flame-tortured spirit is dead.

And look; can that fellow, just five feet eight,
With scarce a beard on his chin,
Can he, too, snatch at the slacks of the rein,
Till he groans as he tightens him in?
He can. And this Vulcan of smoke and of flame,
With such a momentum of will,
Stands at last a grim smoky colossus in steel,
And two rail-lengths of muscle is still.

Ay, call me, the sneer lying deep on your lip,
The paler but cultured ape;
Lord of the brute, with the soul of a brute,
And a cunning to fashion and shape.
I turn from your creed to this miracled deed
We have set on twin pathways of rods;
And I know that the new flings a blush on the old,
And that my fellows are gods.

NOTTMAN

That was Nottman waving at me,
But the steam fell down, so you could not see;
He is out to-day with the fast express,
And running a mile in the minute, I guess.

Danger? none in the least, for the way
Is good, though the curves are sharp as you say,
But bless you, when trains are a little behind,
They thunder around them—a match for the wind.

Nottman himself is a devil to drive,
But cool and steady, and ever alive
To whatever danger is looming in front,
When a train has run hard to gain time for a shunt.

But he once got a fear, though, that shook him with pain,
Like sleepers beneath the weight of a train.
I remember the story well, for, you see,
His stoker, Jack Martin, told it to me.

Nottman had sent down the wife for a change
To the old folks living at Riverly Grange,
A quiet sleepy sort of a town,

Save when the engines went up and down.

For close behind it the railway ran
In a mile of a straight if a single span;
Three bridges were over the straight, and between
Two the distant signal was seen.

She had with her her boy 'a nice little chit
Full of romp and mischief, and childish wit,
And every time that we thunder'd by,
Both were out on the watch for Nottman and I.

"Well, one day," said Jack, "on our journey down,
Coming round on the straight at the back of the town,
I saw right ahead, in front of our track,
In the haze on the rail something dim-like and black.

"I look'd over at Nottman, but ere I could speak,
He shut off the steam, and with one wild shriek,
A whistle took to the air with a bound;
But the object ahead never stirr'd at the sound.

"In a moment he flung himself down on his knee,
Leant over the side of the engine to see,
Took one look, then sprung up, crying, breathless and pale,
'Brake, Jack, it is some one asleep on the rail!'

"The rear brakes were whistled on in a trice
While I screw'd on the tender brake firm as a vice,
But still we tore on with this terrible thought
Sending fear to our hearts—'Can we stop her or not?'

"I took one look again, then sung out to my mate,
'We can never draw up, we have seen it too late.'
When, sudden and swift, like the change in a dream,
Nottman drew back the lever and flung on the steam.

"The great wheels stagger'd and span with the strain,
While the spray from the steam fell around us like rain,
But we slacken'd our speed, till we saw with a wild
Throb at the heart, right before us,—a child!

"It was lying asleep on the rail, with no fear
Of the terrible death that was looming so near;
The sweat on us both broke as cold as the dew
Of death as we question'd—'What can we do?'

"It was done—swift as acts that take place in a dream—

Nottman rush'd to the front and knelt down on the beam,
Put one foot in the couplings; the other he kept
Right in front of the wheel for the child that still slept.

"'Saved!' I burst forth, my heart leaping with pride,
For one touch of the foot sent the child to the side,
But Nottman look'd up, his lips white as with foam,
'My God, Jack,' he cried, 'It's my own little Tom!'

"He shrunk, would have slipp'd, but one grasp of my hand,
Held him firm till the engine was brought to a stand,
Then I heard from behind a shriek take to the air,
And I knew that the voice of a mother was there.

"The boy was all right, had got off with a scratch:
He had crept through the fence in his frolic to watch
For his father; but, wearied with mischief and play,
Had fallen asleep on the rail where he lay.

"For days after that on our journey down,
Ere we came to the straight at the back of the town,
As if the signal were up with its gleam
Of red, Nottman always shut off the steam."

DUNCAN WEIR

Bacl on the wrong line, that was all,
Back in the morning, dusky and drear,
Simple enough such a thing you may call,
But it cost us the life of Duncan Weir.

He was our mate for many a day;
Never a steadier man on the line,
First at his work on the iron way,
Whether the morning was stormy or fine.

Quiet, yet fond of a laugh and a joke,
Though at times he took other moods, and then
He would only look up for a five minutes' smoke,
Then take to the shovel and pick again.

We liked him, for Duncan was kind of heart,
And a kindly heart has a kindly speech,
But one dreary morning put us apart,
And our mate was forever out of our reach.

I was standing that morning a pace from the door,
When up came one of our men and said,
"Ready! for Duncan is on before,"
So we took to the rail with a hasty tread.

But just as we stood on the top of the bank,
Three white lights at once through the darkness burst;
And with steady, oily, monotonous clank,
An engine shot past us with tender first.

I half leapt over the bank as the glare
Of the head-light beckon'd along the track,
Then taking one look—"That is old Tom Blair,
And he's back on the wrong line," I said to Jack.

"Blair?" echoed Jack, and he turn'd to me,
"Yes! for the lamps made his number plain,
He has been to the tank for water, you see,
And come down on the wrong line in front of his train.

"We stood till the engine was out of our view,
Then I felt at my heart the chill touch of a fear;
My mate said nothing, though well I knew,
Like myself he was thinking of Duncan Weir.

For Duncan, who always had ways of his own,
From his very first start on the line, took pains
To walk to and back from his work when alone,
On the four-feet way, with his face to the trains.

We bent with a hasty footstep our way
Down the line, till, at once with a clutch of the hand,
My mate drew me back to where something lay
Dim and dark in the four-feet, just where you stand.

My heart beat fast as I leapt the rail;
One touch was enough, and with wild affright,
I said in a voice that was like to fail,
"My God, it is Duncan; run back for a light."

When the lamp came up, and its light was shed,
Like a great round flashing eye on the place,
There was our old mate Duncan,—dead—
Struck from behind, for he lay on his face.

Well, little was said—just a question or two
At the driver. But all taking place in the dark
Gave him room to deny, so it past from view,

And all that is left is that simple mark.

Just his name on the fence—take a step this way,—
You can see it from here with the day and date,
When old Tom Blair, while the morning was grey,
Came back on the wrong line and kill'd our mate.

THE BROWN GIANT

Hurrah for this rough brown giant of ours!
He stood by the side of God
When the stars were shot from His strong righthand
To the height of their pure abode;
When this grand firm planet we tread upon
Rose upward formless and dim,
And knelt on its knee with its hands in the air
As they sang their morning hymn.

Hurrah for this rough brown giant of ours!
He stood by the side of man
As he rose in the shape of the Master himself,
With a boundless cunning to plan.
Then God said, looking and smiling at each,
And laying His hands on the two,
"Go forth; I have only roughen'd the earth,
I have left the rest for you."

Then the two came forth to this earth of ours,
The giant still led like a child,
And wherever he bent his back the earth
Look'd up in his face and smiled.
And goodly harvests of grain grew up,
And the red swift wine was quaff'd,
Till it warin'd the heart of the giant, who sang
And held his sides, and laugh'd.

Then cities rose up at his magic touch,
Till the earth was like to groan,
For the fair green sod was cut through with a load
Of a million streets of stone.
And a multitudinous tramp of feet
Went surging up and down;
Ho, ho, and the giant leapt up in his glee,
For his muscles had shaped the town!

Then he taught the puppets who stood by his knee

The cunning that slumbers in fire,
Till they bent the iron as willows are bent,
To each shape of their boundless desire;
But his great heart leapt with a bound to his throat,
And his grim brows whiten'd with fear,
When they drew from their gleaming scabbards of fire
The mighty sword and spear.

Then his eyes grew sad with a gloom, and he shrank
Till he scarce could draw his breath,
As he saw, rank'd up in their terrible files,
Men eager for slaughter and death.
But at last when they met like two whirlwinds in hell,
And the spouting blood reek'd red,
With his broad rough hand as a blind on his eyes,
He turn'd in terror, and fled.

Then he sat him down full of black despair,
And he groan'd as he bent his eyes,
For he saw that his very footsteps were red
With the hue that darkens and dyes.
He sat like one from whose veins the tide
Of full strong life had shrunk;
And his long black hair fell down on his face,
While his head on his bosom sunk.

But he sprung to his feet, and he dash'd his hair
At one wild sweep from his brow;
"What a coward," he said, "to sink thus in my dread,
And this planet awaiting me now.
Have I not on my shoulder the finger of God,
As he laid it on that of the man?
If he strikes into pathways that devils have made
I, at least, will stand true to the plan."

So with strong full heart he stood in the mart,
Till up to his very knees
The treasures of earth lay like sunset in heaps,
He was lord of the lordless seas.
"Hurrah, hurrah!" and his breath came quick,
While he shouted aloud in his glee,
"The king with a million men at his beck
Is never a king like me."

But when he struck forth with his strong right hand,
And the temple rose upward on high,
He bared his forehead, and knelt on his knee,
For he knew that his Master was nigh.

He seem'd, as the smile of God fell upon him,
Kneeling and bowing there,
A grand, stern, all miraculous form
Of Labour and Worship at prayer.

But when he stood by the sculptor, and saw
An angel step from the stone,
Or the mighty shape of some god that rose
In its godship calm and alone—
His heart came and went at each deft chisel stroke,
But his brow wore a doubt as he said,
"Here is toil of a higher kind than my own,
Where God steps in in my stead."

He stood by the painter, who, busy with dreams,
And a grand glow lighting his eyes,
Made his canvas a mirror that took in the earth
As a lake takes the stars and the skies.
Or, soaring upward alone with his soul,
Away from the shadow and mist,
Brought down with a brow full of heaven's own light,
The grand pure features of Christ.

He turn'd from the painter and sculptor, who wrought
In the light common men may not see,
And with low voice whisper'd—"The work of the two
Belongs to a higher than me.
There is something divine which is out of my reach,
Yet it may be mine, but, till then,
I know I can stand with no fear of a lord
In the rush of toiling men."

He shaped the bridge till its footstep of stone
Stept over the wave at one stride;
He fashion'd whatever had shadow of use
For man to keep by his side.
The great brown giant look'd at his arms
And his broad brow glisten'd with sweat,
But still, in the depths of his bosom, he felt
There was something to fashion yet.

He stood lost in thought till the light in his eyes
By his broad grim brows was o'ercast,
Then he drew himself up to his height, as he cried,
"I have found my best triumph at last."
Then the smoke of the furnace-fire grew dark,
And the heavens were deaf with the din
Of hammer and anvil, where glowing and swart

The giant was toiling within.

At length, when his task was over, he stood
With his strong arms over his breast,
As if to keep down the wild pride of his heart
That not for one moment could rest.
"Ho, here I have made you a monster of fire!
One whose muscles can shrink not nor fail;"
And, with one wild rush, like a stroke from the gods,
The engine leapt to the rail.

And with three sharp snorts, as a test of his strength,
He bent himself to each load,
Till his black limbs quiver'd, as quiver the veins
When the hot blood leaps in a god;
And wherever he stamp'd with his merciless hoof
The earth, as if terror-struck, said—
"Here is one who will never give heed to the rein
Till he circles my bounds with his tread."

A flush lay like fire on the giant's cheek,
And a deep glow lit up his eye,
As at every heave of the monster's lungs
A column of smoke took the sky.
But when he drew near for a moment to view
The red flame licking his heart,
And coiling and twisting like snakes when they sting
The giant leapt back with a start.

Then a gloom lay like mist on his brow, and he said,
As if doubt had come backward again,—
"I have made them a steed they can harness at will,
What more can I fashion for men?
They may struggle and conquer, the gods of this earth!
Yet whatever their miracles be,
Let them know that the fingers of God are on them,
As I feel them, this moment on me."

Then hurrah for this rough brown giant of ours!
He stood with God in His place
When the stars like a million silver drops
Were hung in the azure of space.
And hurrah! when he came with a firm free step
To stand beside man on the soil,
To head like a Titan Napoleon still
The bloodless battles of toil.

I work upon the line to-day,
The rails on either side of me,
But all my fancies wing their way,
Like swallows flying out to sea.

And ever as they speed, I dream
Of all the coming thousand things
That time will herald with a beam
Of light from off his windless wings:

What changes in the great to Be
Evolving broad, and far, and grand,
What faiths by which our kind shall see
That spinning creeds is spinning sand:

What worlds we dare not dream of now,
When Science with her eagle ken
Holds a white hand above her brow
To bring them nearer unto men:

When all the canker and the pride
Shall sink, and all the good in store
Will work and toil with us, and glide
Like Christ, among the lowly poor:

When war, a red and sulky hell
Upbursting through the green of earth,
Shall sink for ever, but to dwell
In chaos where it first had birth:

When all the lower man is sunk,
To leave him as of old again,
Ere that one taint had made him drunk
With the wild wine that devils drain:

What songs whose melody shall start
The higher music pure and free,
In poets hymning strong of heart
The labour Epics that will be.

Then the great brotherhood of man
Will sing its universal psalm,
And Peace from paradise again
Come smiling underneath the palm.

Ay, speed the time when, strong of breath
And heart that not a fear can quail,
We keep to all the higher faith
As the wild engine keeps the rail:

When, brain and heart no longer twain,
We work—God's sky above us blue—
"Stand clear, man, for that Pullman train,
Not twenty lengths of rail from you!"

I leap aside, the train roars past,
And all my fancies, worn and sick,
Come slowly back, to die at last
In the sharp raspings of the pick.

THE GODS AND THE WINDS

The still gods, though they move apart
From interchange of thoughts with men,
Yearn to come down, and, in the mart,
Rub shoulders with them once again,

And help them in each fearless deed,
When Science with serenest eyes
Lays a white finger on each need,
While Thought springs forward to devise.

"We won our godship far too young,"
They moan with an Immortal's woe;
"Our mighty strength is all unstrung
In shame when we look down below.

"The vigour of our limb is weak,
Our pulses move as with a load,
And only place upon our cheek
That burning spot which shames a god."

The keen winds send their voices up,
They whistle past each lonely star;
The gods pause ere they lift the cup,
As held back by some sudden bar.

"Keep to your halls," the rough winds say,
"Nor overstep your starry pale,
Ye could not for one moment play
With the wild engine on the rail;

"Nor even match, though keen and strong,
And all aglow with swiftest fire,
That silent speed which hurls along
The far word lightnings of the wire.

"For men have bound the giant brain
To use, and with swift hands they bring
Wild untaught things they slowly train,
That after into wonders spring.

"Which, leaping at one bound, the bar
Of use and wont, enclasp the earth,
That trembles at such sudden war,
And reels into its second birth.

"Then life in all its new-found glow
Wakes up, and with a certain hand
Seizes the wand of Prospero,
That magic may be in the land.

"So men dive, in their wild designs,
Far down, and, in the earth's deep night,
Battle until, like slaves, the mines
Pour forth their treasures to the light.

"And great wild engines black with smoke
Roar on along the rail, or urge
With clank, and pant, and sullen stroke,
A thousand riches through the surge.

"So keep your halls, nor fret, nor moan
That ye can never come again,
A second godship is not won
Among these nineteenth century men."

Thus the bold winds against the sky
Uplift their voices wild and strong,—
The gods, still moaning, make reply,
"We won our godship far too young."

STOOD AT CLEAR

"Where is Adams?" that was the cry,
"Let us question him before he die."

Naught around in the night was seen
Save the glimmer of lamps, where the crash had been.

Right across the six-feet way,
One huge hulk, engine and tender lay,

While the wailing hiss of the steam took the air,
By fits, like the low, dull tone of despair.

But still above all, rose that one clear cry
"Speak to Adams before he die."

"Here," I said, "turn your lamps on me,"
And I laid Jim's head upon my knee,

"Jim, old mate," I said in his ear,
They will ask you a question—can you hear?"

Then I saw through the grime that was on his face,
A white hue coming with slow, sure pace;

And upon his brow by the light of the lamp,
Other dew than the night's lay heavy and damp.

"Speak to him-quick!" they bent and said,
"Did the distant signal stand at red?"

Broken and slow came the words with a moan,
"Stood—at—clear," and poor Jim was gone.

I turn'd my head away from the light
To hide the tears that were blinding my sight,

And pray'd from my heart, to God that Jim
Might find heaven's signals clear to him.

OLD WYLIE'S STONE

You want to see Wylie's stone—look here;
But stop where you are till the line is clear;
Pullman express from the south is due,
And will be here in a moment or two.

Here she is, coming round the curve,
Sudden and swift, and with never a swerve;
And a whirl of smoke that you scarce can see,

The driver waving his hand at me.

You see at the foot of the slope down there
That stone from the grass and moss laid bare,
That was the spot where Wylie lay,
When the engine pitch'd him over that day.

We were working here, for the levels change,
And the metals often get out of range:
The wind was high, and we scarce could hear
The trains till they whistled within our ear.

Well, we just had finish'd with our repairs,
And were sorting the ballast about the chairs,
When the afternoon goods, about half-an-hour late,
Came round upon us as steady as fate.

We stood clear of both lines, and were watching the train
Coming up with a full head of steam on the strain,
When all at once one of our men gave a shout—
There's a shovel against the rail! Look out!

The shovel was Wylie's, and swift as a wink,
He sprang into the four feet with never a shrink;
Clutch'd it: but ere he could clear the track,
The buffer beam hit him right in the back.

In a moment poor Wylie was over the slope,
And we after him, but with little of hope;
Found him close by the stone, with his grip firm set
On the shovel that cost him his life to get.

We lifted him up, and as light as we could,
Bore him home to his cot you see over the wood;
Stood by his bed, each with pent-up breath,
As we saw the steady advance of death.

But just ere it came he lifted his hand,
Made a motion we could not but understand,
So we drew nearer to him as he lay,
To hear what our mate had got to say.

"Wylie," I said, and he open'd his eyes,
With a look of faint, far-off surprise;
Then, clasping my hand, he strove to speak,
As his ebbing breath wax'd slow and weak.

At length, as I almost bent my head

To his lips, in a strange weird whisper, he said—
"Call the spot where I lay old Wylie's stone!"
That was all he said, and our mate was gone.

So we call it "Wylie's stone" to this day,
To mark to strangers the spot where he lay;
You can see the very wild flowers from here
Growing round it. We planted them there last year.

THE CUCKOO

Ami the sound of picks to-day,
And shovels rasping on the rail,
A sweet voice came from far away,
From out a gladly greening vale.

My mate look'd up in some surprise;
I half stopp'd humming idle rhyme:
Then said, the moisture in my eyes,
"The cuckoo, Jack, for the first time."

How sweet he sang! I could have stood
For hours, and heard that simple strain;
An early gladness throng'd my blood,
And brought my boyhood back again.

The primrose took a deeper hue,
The dewy grass a greener look;
The violet wore a deeper blue,
A lighter music led the brook.

Each thing to its own depth was stirr'd,
Leaf, flower, and heaven's moving cloud,
As still he piped, that stranger bird,
His mellow May-song clear and loud.

Would I could see him as he sings,
When, as if thought and act were one,
He came; the grey on neck and wings
Turn'd white against the happy sun.

I knew his well-known sober flight,
That boyhood made so dear to me;
And, blessings on him! he stopp'd in sight,
And sang where I could hear and see.

Two simple notes were all he sang,
And yet my manhood fled away;
Dear God! The earth is always young,
And I am young with it to-day.

A wondrous realm of early joy
Grew all around as I became
Among my mates a bearded boy,
That could have wept but for the shame.

For all my purer life, now dead,
Rose up, fair-fashion'd, at the call
Of that grey bird, whose voice had shed
The charm of boyhood over all.

O early hopes and sweet spring tears!
That heart has never known its prime
That stands without a tear and hears
The cuckoo's voice for the first time.

THE DEAD LARK

On the slope, half-hid in grass, and right beneath the sounding wire,
Lay the Lark, the sweetest singer in the Heavenly Father's choir,
Dead, no more to thrill the heavens with his music long and loud,
Coming from the sunny silence, moving on the fleecy cloud.
Tenderly the thing I lifted, smooth'd the ruffle on his breast,
That had still'd the beat of life, and sent his singing soul to rest.
O what melodies unutter'd, lyrics of the happiest praise,
Lay within my hands, forever useless to the summer days.
Then I thought a want would wander, like a strangely jarring tone
Through the singing choir, and only to be mark'd of God alone.
For we muffle up our vision, seeing not for earthly stain
All that He in wisdom fashions for His glory and our gain.
And as still I stood and held him, in the sunshine overhead
Sang and shook his merry fellows, heedless of their brother dead;
Then my heart was stirr'd within me as I heard them at their song,
For I deem'd their touch of music did this little fellow wrong,
And my tears came slowly upward, as a low sweet undertone
Whisper'd to me, "Thus forever sing the thoughtless of thy own.
Far into the realms of Fancy soar they in their sounding flight,
Heeding not below some brother with a wing of feebler might.
Yet the same sweet aspirations throb through all the songs he sings,
And the same deep impulse yearning for the better human things.
But his voice, like sounds in twilight, echoes but to die away,
While the deep heart throbbing in him fain would burst into the day.

But his higher fellows hear not, listen not its earnest tone,
That comes out in simple sound between the pauses of their own,
So he pines away in silence, keeping back the tide of song,
Till the rush and fret within him works at last its end in wrong;
And he, seeing beyond the promise of a better kindred band,
Dies, his bosom full of lyrics, like the lark's within my hand."
Waking up, the day's set labour still'd the fancies in my breast,
So I laid the fallen minstrel into his unnoticed rest,
Left him and the music with him lying in his grassy bed
To the carol of his fellows and the sunshine overhead.

JIM DALLEY

"So you knew Dalley that used to drive
That spanking old engine—fifty-five;"
Knew him? why, Dalley was my mate,
He died beside me upon the plate.

Let me see, it is over two years ago
Since Thorley's cutting was block'd with snow,
What a night was that, and how heavy our shift
To get in with our train through the storm and drift.

But Jim and I did it; we always had luck
To get through, though the rest of our fellows stuck,
Came in with their train about half-a-day late
To learn of the sudden death of my mate.

Brave rough Jim! I can see him to-day
As if he never had pass'd away;
Hear the very sound of his voice as he said,
"Are the junction signals set at red?"

We were out that night on the goods that ran through,
Running sharp, for our speed was what steam could do,
But from time to time, as we look'd behind,
Like a great white sheet came the snow on the wind.

We had just two shunts; the last for the mail—
She was late, for already upon the rail
The snow lay thick, but she thunder'd past
Like a great, red, smoky ghost in the blast.

"Now," said Jim, "we have nothing to fear
If we catch the rest of the signals clear."
So he flung on the steam, and with one loud roar,

We went plunging into the storm once more.

The snow fell on either side, and the wire
Moan'd, as if harping on some desire,
While above, as the furnace threw up its light,
Was a whirling cover of black and white.

The signals glimmer'd a faint green spark,
Far up as if somewhere within the dark,
The engine wheels had a ghostly sound,
As they struck and scatter'd the snow around.

The trains on the up line seem'd to glow
With a misty halo of drift and snow,
While a wave from their drivers as they flew
Was like a wave from a ghost to our view.

But still we tore on with no wish to fail,
Though the great wheels clank'd and slipp'd on the rail;
But I kept up the steam while Jim look'd out
Into the dark with a fear and a doubt.

By this we had left behind Mossley Bank,
And had reach'd the summit at Riverley Jank,
"Down hill after this," I sung over to Jim;
But he stood in his place, never stirring a limb.

At length on his stepping backward a pace
The light of the tube lamp fell on his face,
It was white as if with unspoken fear,
As he turn'd and said, "Bob, come over here."

"Why, what is the matter?" I said, as I stood
Beside him, but Jim was again in the mood
Of staring ahead; at last he awoke,
And laying his hand on my shoulder spoke.

"All the night, Bob, from the time we lay through
For the mail, this sight has been in my view,
And right ahead in the snow I can see
My wife with her youngest upon her knee.

"I see her sitting as if on the wait
For me, and before her a fireless grate,
She is weeping and wringing her hands as in pain;
My God! I wish we were home with our train."

I tried to cheer him, and spoke of his fear

As a whim from which he would soon get clear,
But again he was standing upright in his place,
With the same pale, weary look on his face.

I felt myself shudder as if with a chill,
Or a nameless dread of some coming ill,
But I kept myself up to be ready to catch
The signals my mate was not fit to watch.

What a weary drive through the storm that rung
Before and behind us as onward we swung,
But at last in the distance we caught a gleam,
"Home at last," said Jim, and flung off the steam.

We ran through the points and drew up in the lye,
My mate still gazing ahead, while I,
Glad to think he soon would get rid of his fright,
Leapt off to uncouple our train for the night.

"Now then, old fellow, go on," I cried;
Coming back from the tender—no voice replied,
And looking upward I saw that be leant
Forward against the window half bent.

One moment and I was upon the plate
With my hand on the shoulder of my mate,
"Jim?" No answer, I lifted his head—
Dalley lay over the levers dead.

WHAT THE ENGINE SAYS

What does the mighty engine say,
Rolling along
Swift and strong,
Slow or fast as his driver may,
Hour by hour, and day by day,
His swarthy side
Aglow with pride,
And his muscles of sinewy steel ablaze?
This is what the engine says:

First his breath gives a sudden snort,
As if a spasm had cut it short,
Then with one wild note
To clear his throat,
He fumes and whistles—"Get out of my way,

What are you standing there for—say?
Fling shovel and pick
Away from you, quick!
Ere my gleaming limbs with out-reaching clutch
Draw you into your death with a single touch.
For what care I for a puppet or two,
A little over five feet like you?

I must rush to the city with one long stride,
Add a wave of men to the streets' wild tide,
Bring friends to friends,
And gather the ends
Of all the trailing threads of use,
So that no single ply may be loose,
Run in the front of traffic, and shape
A way for its thousand feet, and fling
This planet into fashioning,
That others unknown to us may ape.
So I say,
Stand clear from the way."

"O, well," I said,
And I shook my head,
But all the while taking care to clear
The way, for the iron fellow so near.
"You carry things just a little too far,
For great, and swarthy, and strong as you are,
With the strength of a hundred Titans within
Your seething breast with its fiery din,
And your iron plates that serve you for skin,
With a single twitch
Of this crow-bar,
I could make you welter within the ditch,
As if Jove himself had open'd war;
So you see
You must pay a little respect to me.
I keep the rail
Tight and firm with chair and key,
Fasten the joints as firm as may be
So that your pathway may not fail.
Why, if I twitch'd a rail from the chairs,
Where would you be? At your smoky prayers,
Lying alone,
With only strength to mutter a groan,
And fifty fellows about my size
Scrambling upon you with shouts and cries,
Till they get you bound up in a coil of chains—
Click goes the jack, and rasp the crane,

What a labour to get you up again!

"Why, when your feet are once clear of the rail,
You're as weak as an infant and as frail;
Now look again,
You are panting and snorting as if in disdain,
For the fever of fire leaps like mad in your breast,
Toiling and seething,
And fuming and breathing,
Yet always bent upon spoiling your rest.
But look at your driver—one touch of his hand
Makes you stop or go on as he likes to command.
Talk of your strength!
Why, not to go to the utmost length,
I could almost blush if I had to speak"—

Here he gives a sudden shriek,
And a wild long bound
That shakes the ground,
Then clearing his dusky throat to speak,
He pauses as if to gather strength,
Then hoarsely thunders out at length:

"So you want me to bow to you,
And to give you praise for the little you do.
Why, if I,
As I thunder by
Thought that you had such a whim in your head,
I would hurl right and left the rails that I tread
In utter contempt of your paltry pride,
That is making you think"—

"Stop a moment," I cried,
"You are taking me up just a little too quick,"
And here I flung down at my feet the pick,
"You are the thought and the force of my kind,
The monster of fire,
Whose boundless desire
Clutches at all—nay, the very mind
Of this iron age
Is heard in your rage.
But here I stand as a help to you,
Proud of the task which I have to do,
Yet a touch of pride made me let you see,
That great as you are you depend on me.
Come, own at once you were hasty and strong,
And I'll sing your terrible strength in a song."

Here he thought for a moment, and then
With a snort and a whistle, his mighty limb
Clutch'd at the rail
That was like to fail,
Then as if thought had come back to him
He cried, "The world and toiling men
Great and small are bound in one chain,
Each must help each or they work in vain;
So here with a whistle I own I was wrong,
And start when you like to sing your song."

That was what the engine said,
With a whoop and a hail
As he kept the rail,
Butting space backward with his head.

THE WIRES

I Lay beneath the long slim wires,
And heard them murmur like desires,
Till, drowsy with the heat, my thoughts
Set out, like errant knights to find
A land of dreams, and sunny spots
That have no visit of the wind,
And as they went, with restless choice,
Lo! the wires above took voice.

First Wire

I bear through the air
Like the breath of despair
Desolation and famine and dread,
For two nations uprising led onward by hate,
Clutch at each other mid heaps of the dead,
While the black lips of cannon belch forth with a yell,
And a hissing that withers and darkens like fate,
The vomit of hell.

Second Wire

Soft and low
Let my message be spoken,
To a mother that hears
With a grief that hath no tears,
How her only son is stricken down
In the wild heart of the reckless town,

Where life is as full as a river's flow,
Then come away,
For who would delay,
When a wailing heart is broken?

Third Wire

I flash to a people over the sea
A mighty truth that will make them free,
For kindred spirits transmit to each
The God-given truths they have sworn to preach.
Death to all tyranny and wrong,
Which poets wither with their song,
Let men be free in the glorious light
Of a brotherhood that sees and smites
The Hydra broods that fain would clutch
The throat of devil-defying Right;
Cut them down, they are nought but blights,
God himself is aweary of such.

Fourth Wire

My message is from one who fled
Long years ago. They thought him dead,
So in their hearts they dug a grave,
And laid in thought therein their boy,
He is coming home to clasp their hands:
I almost feel from here their joy.

Fifth Wire

A sudden and great commercial crash
Like a current of doom is in my flash,
And thousands will put their hands to-day
On a bubble that winds will blow away.

Sixth Wire

A sound of bells is in my tone,
Of marriage bells so glad and gay,
It comes straight from the heart of one
A thousand weary miles away.
O sweet to see in a foreign land
An English bride by the altar stand,
Her eyelids wet with tears that seem
Like dews that herald some sweet dream,
As, blushing, she falters forth the "yes,"
That opens a world of happiness;

But hush, this is all I have got to say—
"Harry and I were married to-day."

Seventh Wire

I rush in the very front of time
With a finger pointing at sudden crime,
The fool! when the deed was done and he stood
Looking down at his hands, that were red with blood,
Never thought for a single moment on me,
But my mark was on him as he turn'd to flee.

Eighth Wire

I fling on men a sudden gloom and pain,
In quiet hamlet and in toiling town,
Their greatest and their noblest man is down;
Death conquers; but his triumph is in vain.
For as I flash the news, as one draws breath
But swifter, so the dead man's Christ-like aim
Will flash like fire into their hearts, and claim
A newer meaning from this touch of death.

The voices ceased, and half dreaming still
In the drowsy shade of the slope, I thought
"Eight wires have murmur'd their good and ill—
There are nine, but the ninth has spoken not;
What can the burden be of its rhyme
When it speaks?" and I had not long to wait.

Ninth Wire

Limited mail is sharp at her time,
But the Pullman is twenty minutes late.

BOB CRUIKSHANKS

This is what Bob Cruikshanks said,
With a doubtful shake of the head,
And an oily hand that began to feel
Round the fringes of his beard so red,
As he leant against the driving-wheel.

"In the roar of the engine upon the rail,
Which I dimly feel
Underneath my heel,

Lurks the music of that which I always fail
To put into fitting words, though I hear
The great song humming within my ear.

"It begins when I start, and it follows on,
It mingles and finds
A home in the winds,
Who catch and toy with its rough, wild tone.
It never ceases, for when we come
To a stand it sinks to a softer hum.

"And often when roaring and rushing along
I can fancy I see
That wild melody
Resting on every spot like a throng
Of tiny spirits that sing and shake
With joy at the things that men will make.

"When I lean myself over the side to watch
The cranks, I know
That somewhere below
In the network of rods there is one to catch
The music they make, which he sings again
To the monster who lets me hold the rein.

"I hear it wild and weird as we skim
Along the bridge,
Or close by the edge
Of some chasm whose jaws open rugged and grim,
As if to swallow the engine, if he
Should prove false to the touch of the rail or me.

"It roars in the tunnel, it gleams in the night,
And with wild desire
From the furnace fire
Leaps sudden and swift with the column of light
That shoots to the clouds in its frenzy to win
Fresh food for the flame that is seething within.

"It whirls with the smoke; it takes up to the air
In the whistle that speaks
Its stern watchword, and shrieks,
As if half given over at times to despair;
Nay, it even twines itself round the wheel
Till the mighty rim staggers and seems to feel.

"It waves from the mist looming up like a wall
On each side as we peer

To catch signals at clear;
It flares from the head-light that swims like a ball
Of wan, dim light, or the eye of a ghost,
With its shadowy form in the darkness lost.

"Is it the wailing spirit of steam
Still following on,
With a wild, drear moan,
Its mighty first-born? or a voice from the dream
Of the things that will be when the years display
The wild results which we shape to-day?

"It is something like this which I fancy I hear
In the roar of the wheel
Underneath my heel,
As we dash through space in our wild career;
But to put it into words, you see,
Is the thing just now which is puzzling me."

That was what Bob Cruikshanks said,
With an oily hand that still would feel
Round the fringes of his beard so red,
While the other felt for a pipe which he
Lit, with a shake of his head at me,
As he leant against the driving-wheel.

THE VIOLET

On the down line, and close beside the rail,
A tender violet grew,
A sister spirit, when the stars grew pale,
Gave it a drink of dew.

And so its azure deepen'd day by day,
And sweet it was to see,
As I went up and down the four-feet way,
The flower peep up at me.

I grew to like it—such a tiny thing,
So free from human stains,
Bending and swaying to each rush and swing
Of passing pitiless trains.

And when we came at times to make repair
Beside the place, I took
A living heed to let it blossom there,

To cheer me with its look.

For fancy working in its quiet ways,
Sometimes would change the flower
Into a maiden of these iron days,
When might was right and power.

And up and down the lints of gleaming rail
With echoing clank and shock,
Rode the stern engines in their suits of mail,
Like knights with spears of smoke.

I crown'd her queen of beauty at their call,
And as I knelt beside
My bud, it look'd up, as if knowing all,
And shook with modest pride.

Then restless fancy changing, it became
A martyr firm and high,
Bound to the stake and lick'd with tongues of flame,
With bigots scowling nigh.

Next, a young poet with his soul aglow
With passionate dreams of truth,
And thoughts akin to those that angels know,
Who have eternal youth.

A nature all unfitted for the time,
Born but to droop and fade,
Like long sweet cadences of fairy rhyme
Within the summer shade.

All these and more my little flower did seem,
As to and fro I went,
Not early light or when the sun's soft beam,
That to the west half spent.

It made itself a presence in my thought,
Seen of the inner eye,
So pure and sweet, and yet so near the spot
Where wild trains thunder by.

But one sweet morning, when the young sunshine
Laid long soft arms of light
Around the earth, I found the flower of mine
Stricken as with some blight.

For like a fallen spot of heaven grown pale,

It lent its drooping head
Against the cold touch of the careless rail,
Wither'd, and shrunk, and dead.

Thus some rare soul, toiling for purer gains,
Sinks in the night alone,
While the hoarse world, like the iron trains,
Unheeding, thunders on.

The swart smoke gem with his heart aglow,
And all his giant strength and vigour strung,
To help our toiling lower gods below—
He still remains unsung.

I have but caught, in leaping to the side
To let him pass in smoke and thunder, dim,
Faint half-heard echoes from that rushing tide,
Of song which follows him.

But the keen years that for our coming kind,
Keep greater triumphs than to-day we claim,
Will bring a poet in whose heart the wind
Of song will leap like flame.

He, born into a richer newer time,
And with a wealthier past behind, will sing,
Our wild fire-monster blurr'd with smoke and grime,
Traffic's sole lord and king:

In music worthy of that soul of fire,
Which in him glows and leaps
Like lightnings, ere they cleave in sullen ire
Some jagged cloud that sweeps

The hills in muttered fear. My own dim song
Will fade and sink, as sinks a fitful wind,
Before the grander music, wild and strong
Of him who comes behind.

Alexander Anderson – A Concise Bibliography

A Song of Labour & Other Poems (1873)

The Two Angels & Other Poems (1875)
Songs of the Rail (1878)
Ballads and Sonnets (1879)
Later Poems (1912)

www.ingramcontent.com/pod-product-compliance
Lightning Source LLC
Chambersburg PA
CBHW021940040426
42448CB00008B/1161